My
Servant
Job

My Servant Job

A Discussion Guide on the Wisdom of Job

MORRIS A. INCH

283
BAKER BOOK HOUSE
Grand Rapids, Michigan

Contents

Acknowledgment

I have lost track of the many who, at one point or another, contributed to the development of the manuscript for this book by sharing some insight or rendering some service. I express my appreciation to them all by acknowledging one of their number—Roger Lundin, first a student and now a fellow faculty member. Out of his experience with life he shared with me the suffering it entails and the wisdom and compassion that can be developed as we allow God to work with us in life's crucible. I express my thanks to him and the others he represents—they are contemporary examples of those who reflect the wisdom that makes the paradigm of Job so challenging.

Preface

We generally treat the Book of Job as a commentary on suffering, but it is much more than that. *Pain* certainly rushes to the forefront (both as physical affliction and mental anguish), but *wisdom* is the more persisting subject.

"Have you considered My servant Job?" inquired the Almighty, "for there is no one like him on the earth, a blameless and upright man, fearing God and turning away from evil" (1:8). Not once does God say: "Look at the poor, miserable wretch, so destitute and forsaken." It is not that Job's suffering goes without notice, but that a greater truth unfolds before us. We learn more from God's excited estimate of the sage than from man's dour explorations into his torments. We shall look over the Almighty's shoulder, to see where His finger points, to appreciate what provoked His enthusiasm, to benefit from His direction.

1

As *the* World Turns

Goal: To see life in
general, and suffering in
particular, with God's gracious
purpose for man.

And the Lord said to
Satan, "From where do you come?"
Then Satan answered the Lord and
said, "From roaming about
on the earth and walking
around on it" (Job 1:7).

Where had Satan been? Trudging about the world.
What had he been doing? Observing what some have
called a jungle, where persons struggle against the elements and with one another, only to succumb in the end.
For the moment the stronger appear to prevail at the
expense of those weaker than themselves, but all too soon

they perish as well, leaving the scene for others to play the predictable game of life all over again.

Alternative Perspectives

Such seems to be Satan's appraisal of life. When asked by God as to whether he had considered righteous Job, the adversary impugned: "Does Job fear God for nothing? Hast Thou not made a hedge about him and his house and all that he has, on every side? Thou hast blessed the work of his hands, and his possessions have increased in the land" (1:9-10). Even the tiger leaves off stalking his prey when his stomach has been filled. But take away the animal's provision and see how quickly his temper turns. You think that Job is upright because he gives thanks at a table groaning with choice foods. Ha! Strip his table bare and drive him out of the village. Then you will see how quickly the jungle instincts take over.

God agreed to the test. Let Job lose all that he cherishes and takes pleasure in. Let us find out if life adds up for him to anything more than a jungle.

Previously, Job had been blessed with seven sons and three daughters, and his property was enlarged to the point that he was considered "the greatest of all the men of the east" (1:3). Now all that changed quickly. A messenger arrived with an alarming report: "The oxen were plowing and the donkeys feeding beside them, and the Sabeans attacked and took them. They also slew the servants with the edge of the sword, and I alone have escaped to tell you."

While the first man was still speaking another burst into the room with continuing bad news: "The fire of God fell from heaven and burned up the sheep and the servants and consumed them; and I alone have escaped to tell you."

Before he had finished his account a third arrived to say: "The Chaldeans formed three bands and made a raid on the camels and took them and slew the servants with the edge of the sword; and I alone have escaped to tell you."

On his heels came still a fourth with the most disconcerting word of all: "Your sons and your daughters were eating and drinking wine in their oldest brother's house, and behold, a great wind came from across the wilderness and struck the four corners of the house, and it fell on the young people and they died; and I alone have escaped to tell you" (1:14-19).

Job had no time to recover from one tragedy to the next, each blow landing before the preceding one could be absorbed. At last the messengers retired from the room leaving Job alone. How long he may have sat there too shocked to move we cannot say, but soon he arose, rent his robe, shaved his head, and cast himself to the ground. In his despair he yet worshiped rather than rejected the Almighty. He cried out, saying:

> Naked I came from my mother's womb,
> And naked I shall return there.
> The Lord gave and the Lord has taken away,
> Blessed be the name of the Lord (1:21).

Through all of this disheartening experience Job had not given up on God. Life was for him a cathedral—a place of worship, not a jungle.

The scene shifts once more, and we find Satan returning from another inspection tour. "Have you considered My servant Job?" the Almighty again inquires. "For there is no one like him on the earth, a blameless and upright man fearing God and turning away from evil. And he still holds fast his integrity, although you incited Me against him, to ruin him without cause."

Satan remains unconvinced: "Skin for skin! Yes, all that a man has he will give for his life. However, put forth Thy hand, now, and touch his bone and flesh; he will curse Thee to Thy face." (2:3–5). Life still adds up to a jungle. So what if the cubs perish as long as the tiger remains healthy and strong? A hide for a hide; Job's piety for God's indulgence.

The Almighty allows the trial to go a step further, to infringe on Job's good health as well. Abruptly the sage breaks out with boils from the soles of his feet to the crown of his head. His body seemed to be burning up (30:30). Intense itching accompanied the fever (2:8), and a musty, rancid odor escaped from the sores clustered over his body. Job's appetite failed under such adverse circumstances. Soon his body hung limp on its frame, his eyes sunk back into his head, and his ribs rippled against the skin. His features revealed a horrible caricature of his former appearance (19:20; 2:12).

Had the jungle mentality triumphed at last? So Satan seems to have anticipated, and Job's wife seems to conclude. "Curse God," she urged, "and die!"

Nevertheless, the sage remained resolute: "You speak as one of the foolish women speaks. Shall we indeed accept good from God and not accept adversity?" (2:9–10). Job had not left his cathedral for the jungle.

Jungle or cathedral, these are the alternative views of life. Shall it be survival of the fittest or service to God and to one's fellow man? We must choose between them.

Succeeding ages may recast the options but each persists in its latest form. Joseph Haroutunian describes the jungle mentality as viewed today: "Men are estranged from one another and lost in the crowds of our urban society. They resent not being treated as human beings, and take vengeance by using others for their interest. They care not for community but for getting ahead of others, not for truth but for advantage, not for justice but for their 'rights.' "[1] There you have the savage contemporary, manipulating or being manipulated, destroying or being destroyed.

Scripture does not deny that men live according to the jungle code. Paul stated that he "fought with wild beasts at Ephesus" (I Cor. 15:32). But Job seems inclined toward an alternative, where life resembles a cathedral. It is to this possibility that we are drawn by the question, "Have you considered My servant Job?"

C. S. Lewis clarified the perspective of life as a cathedral when he wrote: "In the fallen and partially redeemed world we may distinguish 1) the simple good descending from God, 2) the simple evil produced by rebellious creatures, and 3) the exploitation of that evil by God for His redemptive purpose, which produces 4) the complex good to which accepted suffering and repented sin contribute."[2] We shall explore this point of view in some detail.

Simple Good

The first ingredient Lewis identifies is the simple good descending from God. "Every good thing bestowed and every perfect gift is from above, coming down from the Father of lights, with whom there is no variation, or shifting shadow" (James 1:17). God's goodness toward us remains constant, whether by day or night.

That simple good originates with God indicates: 1) all that comes from God is good, and 2) all good comes from

God. Only good derives from God and never evil. An appreciation of that truth is the first step toward perceiving life as a cathedral.

Only good derives from God. This important and fundamental truth was maligned by Satan's deceit. Hear him say to Eve concerning the forbidden fruit: "You shall not die! For God knows that in the day you eat from it your eyes will be opened, and you will be like God, knowing good and evil" (Gen. 3:4–5). Satan falsely implied to Eve that the Almighty did not mean the injunction for *her good* but for the protection of *His privilege.*

Satan sowed the seed of doubt concerning the unqualified goodness of God to man. He sowed and it took root. "Does He really have my best interests at heart?" we ask. We must overcome this temptation to doubt if we are to realize life as a cathedral.

The second implication of simple good is that all good comes from God. No other ultimate sources of good exist. And we err by looking elsewhere. For instance, take the person disillusioned by the hypocrisy of others. "Forget them and forget God," he says in disgust, and sets out to achieve a moral life on his own. He fails to understand that even the degree of success he may achieve is a result of the gracious provision of God.

It comes as a surprise to many that the good they experience in life emanates from God, or that they can most fully appreciate it by cultivating a relationship with Him. "To many people conscience is almost all that they have by way of knowledge of God. This still small voice that makes them feel guilty and unhappy before, during, or after wrong-doing, is God speaking to them. . . . It is this which impels them to shoulder the irksome duty and choose the harder path."[3] But God does not resemble the resident policeman as much as a gracious benefactor. He spends less time pointing an accusing finger than sharing the good things of life with us (John 3:17).

As a case in point, I received Christ when a young man in the armed service. Before that time I had experienced many good things—the love of parents, friendships, happy times, and needed lessons. How was I to interpret these good things? My first inclination was to credit them to Satan as part of his plan of deception, and too long this thought persisted with me. But we give Satan more than his due by attributing whatever good we experience to him. He may, in fact, twist the good to fit his purpose, but the good, the simple good, comes from God. Now looking back on those years, I recall the good things as engineered by God, as intimation of His care, and as gracious signposts pointing me toward Himself.

All that comes from God is good, and all good comes from God. With this perception, the first building block for seeing life as a cathedral has been put in place. We may now proceed with the second.

Simple Evil

Lewis couples with the simple good descending from the heavenly Father the simple evil produced by rebellious creatures. An idealistic Curé once addressed a vindictive Comptesse: "Hell is not to love any more, madame. Not to love any more! That sounds quite ordinary to you. To a human being still alive, it means to love less or love elsewhere."[4] The Comptesse was fond of theological speculations but slow to see their practical implications. She theorized about the hell to be, while contributing to the hellishness that is. The zealous Curé tried to shock her back to reality, to see the alienation about her, and how her hatefulness contributed to it.

The Curé had observed that "Hell is to love less or love elsewhere." More to our point, he could have said that "Sin is to love less or love elsewhere." What do we mean by describing sin as loving less? Jesus taught: "You shall love the Lord your God with all your heart, and with all your soul, and with all your mind, and with all your strength," and "you shall love your neighbor as yourself" (Mark 12:30–31). It is with *all* our heart, *all* our soul, *all* our mind, *all* our strength, and with the *full* measure of our self-esteem. Sin amounts to doing less than that.

Sin also means loving elsewhere. J. B. Phillips comments, "A lot of people have no sense of sin at all because they've managed, so far, to keep God at arm's length."[5] They may feel guilty and be morbidly preoccupied with the thought of sin but thoroughly miss the point. Sin means first and foremost a disaffection from God. Man has lost his first love.

Love God. Jesus taught: "He who loves father or mother more than Me is not worthy of Me; and he who loves son or daughter more than Me is not worthy of Me; and he who does not take his cross and follow after Me is not worthy of Me" (Matt. 10:37–38). He made it eminently clear that we are to respond to God and in doing so put the remainder of life in order.

No one should deny the reality of sin understood as loving less and elsewhere, with too little concern for God and others, and too much concern for matters that blunt our sensitivities. At the heart of any honest self-appraisal is the confession, "I have sinned." Yes, I have done those things which should not have been done, and left undone the things to be done. The simple evil of man stands in contrast to the simple good of God.

Redemptive Purpose

We have, in addition,"the exploitation of evil by God for His redemptive purpose." Exploitation of evil? How strange to think that God utilizes evil for His redemptive purpose! Strange, but true.

After we have recovered from the initial shock of picturing God working good out of evil, we want to discover how He does it. How can the Almighty turn simple evil to serve His purpose?

Caught up in personal rationalization and social acceptance, sin takes on an unwarranted respectability. Think about the case of a thoughtless critic. He gets a certain satisfaction over inflating his ego at the expense of others. He drops a snide remark here and adds a bit of sarcasm there, all the while convincing himself that no harm will result. The more he exercises his evil tongue, the less he senses the hurt to others or the callousness building within himself.

He also receives encouragement for his behavior. There are always those who will lend their approval with an appreciative laugh or an added comment of their own. And somehow sin seldom seems as bad when others join in.

So the heedless critic blunders along until interrupted by one providential circumstance or another. Perhaps a woman breaks into tears as a result of his insinuation or a man lashes back so viciously as to shake his complacency. Then, in a moment which seems like an eternity, the terrible truth awakens within him. The weight of guilt grips him as if it would crush life itself from his body. God has turned simple evil into the realization of personal need.

Just as the Almighty uses our sin to accent guilt so also does He employ it to reveal His grace. Picture the previously mentioned man now overcome with remorse. Somewhere back in his consciousness a verse of Scripture, committed to memory in his youth, begins to make its way through the maze of memory. It arrives like a sweet refrain to a troubled mind:

"Come now, and let us reason together,"
Says the Lord,
"Though your sins are as scarlet,
They will be as white as snow;
Though they are red like crimson,
They will be like wool" (Isa. 1:18).

The man concludes that God has not only taken his sin to accent his guilt but also to lead him to experience grace.

The experience of God's grace implies not only pardon but power. The repentant critic discovers as he relies upon the Almighty that he can cope with the problems he has created, his perverse companions, and his own evil inclinations. When he has been enabled to turn from what displeased God, harmed others, and tormented self, then evil has contributed most fully to God's redemptive purpose. The perception of life as a jungle takes another step backward, and we can see a cathedral rising overhead.

Complex Good

The simple good of the Creator plus the simple evil of the creature plus the redemptive purpose of God equal the complex good, to which accepted suffering and repented sin contribute. Lewis's equation now stands complete.

Lewis further explains that our acceptance of suffering contributes to the complex good. It is not suffering per se but the way in which we approach suffering. The Scrip-

ture consistently treats pain as undesirable, representing
it in connection with travail (I Sam. 4:19; Isa. 21:3; 66:7),
the devastation of war (Ps. 55:4; Joel 2:6), taxing labor (II
Cor. 11:27), sickness and death (Job 33:19; Ps. 116:3), and
general testing (James 1:2–3; I Peter 1:6–7). As unpleasant as the prospect of pain may be, it often suggests some
greater good to be achieved as a result. So Jesus observed,
"Whenever a woman is in travail she has sorrow, because
her hour has come; but when she gives birth to the child,
she remembers the anguish no more, for joy that a child
has been born into the world" (John 16:21). The image of
travail and birth is a good way to say that "pain is not bad
when it warns us of a serious injury and is not evil if it
provides a service to man in his situation."[6] In fact, the
absence of pain under such circumstances would be unfortunate and could be disastrous.

For example, a man who has been working too hard, too
long, and under severe emotional stress reaches across
his desk and a sharp pain pierces his chest. He draws a
deep breath and steadies himself as a second and more
severe spasm constricts him. Then, after successfully
fighting his way back from a heart attack, he finally begins
to take his doctor's warning seriously, and his life on earth
is extended.

Or consider another example. Only after someone experiences hunger for himself will that painful memory
make him a more compassionate person thereafter. When
pain warns us of a problem or primes us to serve others,
then suffering can contribute to the complex good.

Lewis adds that repented sin likewise serves. He explains: "A merciful man aims at his neighbour's good and
so does 'God's will,' consciously co-operating with 'the
simple good.' A cruel man oppresses his neighbour, and
so does simple evil. But in doing such evil, he is used by
God, without his own knowledge or consent, to produce

the complex good—so that the first man serves God as a son, and the second as a tool."[7] The important distinction between a son and a tool can be thought of in the following fashion. Suppose an engineer seeks to secure a building right-of-way. He finds that there are a few who desire to be of help and are even willing to surrender lesser interests to see his project succeed. But there are others who intend to obstruct his endeavor. He will take both into consideration in his overall design, but the former are what Lewis refers to as *sons* and the latter are *tools*.

The difference between sons and tools when reduced to one word is *repentance*. The sons surrender their obstructionist role to cooperate with the purpose of God.

The final stone has now been fitted into the cathedral's superstructure. Left behind is the jungle and its code of survival of the fittest. We have entered into a perspective where worship is the order of the day. Listen again to Job's words, "Shall we indeed accept good from God and not adversity?" His answer to this rhetorical question certainly comes as no surprise. Of course we can accept adversity, suffering, or whatever comes our way, knowing that God turns such matters to serve His redemptive purpose. Life in general, and pain in particular, are subsumed under the complex good, not the simple good that God sends but the complex good that captures even man's worst and leads it captive to the Victor.

Both the jungle and cathedral perspectives persist, depending on the viewpoint of the individual. The one compounds our difficulty, and the other eases it immeasurably. The former makes life harder to bear, but the latter brings consolation and meaning to life.

"Have you considered My servant Job? For there is no one like him on the earth, a blameless and upright man, fearing God and turning away from evil." Have you witnessed how he lives in a cathedral raised in the midst of a jungle? Start with the simple good, face honestly the fact of simple evil, push on as God exploits evil for His redemptive purpose, and wrap it all together with the complex good, to which suffering and repented sin contribute. Do not expect this to be a simplistic formula but consider it a broad guideline to an abundant life. Anticipate that the perspective will be shaken through testing, but hang on to it. Expect that God will honor your trust.

Questions for Study and Discussion

1. What are the implications for life depending on whether we think of it as a jungle or cathedral? How does Job illustrate the latter alternative?

2. Paul traces man's fault from the fact that "even though they knew God, they did not honor Him as God, or give thanks" (Rom. 1:21a). In what ways does this observation tie into the discussion of the simple good and simple evil? Does it have relevance for any other of the topics considered?

3. How adequate is the idea of sin as loving less or loving elsewhere? What are some of the false views of sin? Can this idea be of help in correcting these false views?

4. Scripture reads, "For those whom the Lord loves He disciplines, and He scourges every son whom He receives" (Heb. 12:6). What do you understand this text to mean? How might you use it in regard to someone who is suffering or to another whose life has been strikingly free from pain?

5. What is involved in the distinction between sons and tools? How does one give up the one in preference for the other?

6. "Through all this Job did not sin nor did he blame God" (1:22). What does it mean to blame God for something that has happened? How does this verse summarize Job's response to the events that had transpired? How does it summarize our discussion of those events?

2

Lead on Living

Goal: To discover
in what manner all of life
may contribute to our spiritual
enrichment and growth.

Then his wife said
to him: "Do you still hold fast
your integrity? Curse God
and die" (Job 2:9).

Though Job's wife advocated death for her suffering spouse, he clung tenaciously to life. She could see no purpose to her husband's life under such trying circumstances, but Job believed that even such difficult times could be of some significance. He anticipated the confidence of a later Hebrew, "And we know that God causes all things to work together for good to those who love God, to those who are called according to His purpose" (Rom. 8:28). *All* things work together for good to

those who trust their lives to the Almighty's keeping. Job
mused, "Shall we receive good from God and shall we not
accept adversity?"

We can readily appreciate the wife's feeling for we, too,
are often tempted to reach the same conclusion. A particularly trying experience comes along and we back off,
sulk away from God, shirk our responsibilities, and become embittered with life. We fail to see the development as part of God's providential plan and a means to
help us reap the rich bounty of life.

We would do better to assume Job's perspective—to
discover the implication of accepting all of life as poten-
tially instructive, enriching, and edifying. Rather than
angrily shaking our fists at God, we should open our
hands to receive all that He means to provide for us
through the vicissitudes of life.

Image-Bearer

Once revered as the richest and wisest of men, Job now
retreated to an ash heap. He wrestled with the burning
question as to what life is all about. He pondered what
values may persist apart from favorable circumstances
and the acclaim of others.

We look for some significance to man that is not depen-
dent on a fortuitous order of events. We probe for a deeper
meaning than dictated by one set of conditions or another.
And thus we come to the observation by Dietrich
Bonhoeffer, "Man's being-free-for God and the other person and his being-free-from the creature in his dominion
over it is the image of God in the first man."[1] Here we
have the human factor that remains unshaken by the
changing experiences of life and a more durable insight
than we can obtain from seeing man in any particular set
of circumstances.

God created the world and it was good, but it did not adequately reflect His nature. There was no creature to share His creative freedom, not until man was created for this purpose.

God created man with a freedom that resembled His own. Yet, it was also different. Man was free as a result of the creation and at the disposition of the Creator. God declared, "Let us make man in our image," and it was done.

Man could no more possess freedom than he could bring it into being. Freedom was never given to man in the sense that he could exercise it on his own. But for God sustaining man in his freedom, he inevitably slips into slavery.

Jesus seems to have this in mind when He declares that "every one who commits sin is the slave of sin" (John 8:34). Those listening to Him prided themselves on being Abraham's offspring and "never yet enslaved to any one." How little they understood the tenuous nature of freedom!

"If therefore the Son shall make you free, you shall be free indeed" (John 8:36). Genuine liberty consists of bondage to the will of God. All else is slavery in disguise.

A new dimension to Adam's life came with the creation of Eve. Although Adam's ultimate significance was to be found in relation to God, this could no longer be considered in a solitary fashion. Adam and Eve stood together before the Almighty. He was *their* God and not simply *his* or *her* God.

This suggests that we ought not to think of God as a partisan deity. He does not favor the welfare of one over another. His concern extends equally to all.

Therefore, we should not expect to be treated differentially. As Peter confessed, "I most certainly understand now that God is not one to show partiality, but in every nation the man who fears Him and does what is right, is welcome to Him" (Acts 10:34–35). Or as the King James Version states it, "God is no respecter of persons."

Also, a reciprocal relationship existed between Adam and Eve. They were to have a mutual ministry in giving to and receiving from the other. Neither could live in isolation from this point onward. Their lives would intertwine of necessity.

Jesus told of a rich man who ignored a pathetic beggar at his gate (Luke 16:19–31). In the life to come, he experienced torment for having violated the sacred trust of life—as conditioned by the presence and need of others. Man was intended to share life with God and his fellow man. He was meant to experience communion, to hold things in common with others. The moment he tries to grasp things for himself alone, he breaks the code by which all must live.

Bonhoeffer describes another aspect of creation as well. Not only was man supposed to relate to God and others, he was also to rule over the extended creation. He was to exercise dominion of the creation as a faithful steward of God.

All too often we rob the good earth through selfish indulgence. We forget that "being free from created things is not the ideal freedom of the spirit from nature. This freedom of dominion directly includes our tie to the creatures who are ruled. The soil and the animals whose Lord I am are the world in which I live, without which I am not."[2] That is, man participates in the creation he supervises. If he pollutes the air or poisons the vegetation and wildlife, he thereby endangers himself. There is no freedom from life apart from responsibility for the created order. Man's dominion over the earth involves a stewardship to God for his and its welfare.

How does man's life in all its endless variety contribute to man's spiritual development? When it helps us to realize our relationship to God and others and our responsibility for creation. These are the meaningful aspects of life that remain constant in any circumstance. They focus any given situation on the abiding role of man in God's world.

For God

How does this thesis work out in connection with Job? Earlier, the patriarch was described as the most prominent figure in view: devout, respected, prosperous, and honored. Men marked his presence and waited on his counsel. God seemed to smile upon his every effort. Then, all at once, Job's world caved in.

What happened to Job as the result of these reverses? "God's testing of Job is obviously a threat to Job's initial religiosity. It brings about a radical change of attitude and understanding in Job. Because he is passionately involved in his perplexities, Job finally experiences a deep spiritual upset and illumination, but not before his original moral and religious resources are completely exhausted."[3] The patriarch's faith did not simply slow down—it sputtered, choked, and jerked this way and that, before Job could pull himself away from the crisis.

One author complains, "It is not clear why God, if he is all-powerful, could not have created spiritually significant people in the first place."[4] But it *is* eminently clear why God cannot do so. "Spiritually significant" people are the end product of life lived together and under what are sometimes the most trying of experiences. It is a contradiction of terms to talk about spiritually significant people while denying the occasion for them to develop.

If the issue were still in doubt, we need only turn to

Jesus' own experience. We read that He did not covet
divine immunities but entered fully into human life, even
to include the crucifixion (Phil. 2:6–8). *All* of life played
its part in God's providential plan, like the blending notes
of instruments in some grand orchestration.

Tempted in the wilderness, Jesus pressed on into the
ministry assigned to Him. Meeting the opposition of the
religious establishment, He held to the course. Forsaken
by the disciples, He would not forsake the heavenly
Father. The victim of hate, He loved those who abused
Him. Take a cross-section of Jesus' earthly life at any
point and you discover that He lived it to the full, open to
all the possibilities it had to offer.

The most critical aspect of life is getting to know God
better. The other conditions are relatively incidental;
God is the subject of life. We can learn many random
matters but never get to life's essence unless we come to
know its creator.

The analogy from human relationships, while limited,
is the best way to appreciate the importance of orienting
life toward the Almighty. Suppose we have come to know
some thoroughly inspiring person. Perhaps we witnessed
a doctor in his skill of a delicate operation and sensed the
single devotion that had gone into his preparation. But
that one instance did not suffice. It merely excited us with
the prospect of getting to know him better. We want to
find out how he reacts in other situations, and each time
we see him respond, it reveals some new insight into how
life may be better lived.

If we put such high value on our association with
another human, how much greater value we should place
on a continuing relationship with God. We observe how
He reacts to one challenge and then another, to adversity
as well as success, in all the varied circumstances of life.

Anything less would rob us of valuable insights into the nature of God and subsequently into ourselves as well.

The point is that we are created in *His* image. My youngest son had a whistle that sounded remarkably like a bird, and one could imagine that a bird had been released in the house. But the boy was not created in the bird's image. And he will not find the ultimate meaning of life in dwelling on the flight of our privileged friends. We are formed in God's image, and unless we learn from Him, we shall never genuinely understand ourselves.

Moreover, we cannot expect to associate with God as casual observers. We must get involved with the Almighty and in His concerns. We need to become participants in God's undertaking, because life can never be lived by proxy.

For Others

We must also learn what it means to live for others. Life for God and life for others go together. One is actually impossible without the other.

Job illustrates this additional aspect of life as well as the previous one. For a long time he and his friends sat in silence. Perhaps, given the situation, that was the best thing to have done. Often we talk when there is nothing appropriate to say. But subsequent events suggest that this particular silence resulted more from the dissonance between Job and the others than a sense of fellowship.

What could the patriarch have said to help his insensitive audience? Life seldom provides us with ready-made answers. Nonetheless, experience is meant to be shared, even and perhaps most when it is tormented with pain. There is no virtue to stoic separation from others.

Wayne Oates observes that "sharing implies the open-

ing of selves to one another in trust and confidence."[5]
That is seldom easy to do, especially when experiencing
adversity and self-doubt. The circle of friends constituted
a challenge to Job, one which must have appeared an
added burden to an already desperate situation.

Oates adds to his earlier observation, "The struggle for
maturity is, at the heart of its meaning, the thrust of the
total person in the ceaselessly changing and growing
experience of relating oneself abidingly to other people
and to God."[6] It is never a task to be set aside for reason of
some previous success or failure. Job had to find a way to
break through the silence that engulfed him, to draw
others into his confidence.

Job may have started to speak from time to time, only to
refrain in the end. It may have seemed too difficult in
addition to bearing his suffering. Or he was uncertain as
to the response of his friends. Or he surmised that there
was little to be gained by the interchange. And when Job
finally broke the silence and received such an insensitive
response, he probably had second thoughts.

Nonetheless, life amounts to being available to others,
even when we face adversity. We recall how Jesus ex-
pressed concern for His mother as He suffered upon the
cross. He also asked forgiveness for those afflicting Him.
And He offered hope for the penitent thief. He did not cut
Himself off from others.

When Job broke the silence it was in principle a victory. He thereby acknowledged the presence of others
and their claim upon him. He also permitted God to work
through them on his behalf. We must appreciate his effort
not in terms of the frustrating dialogue that followed but
the end result—when God put all that had previously
transpired into proper perspective.

Somewhere, not yet in sight for Job, lay the deeper

realization of what God was bringing to pass. His suffering, the callousness of his friends, and the uncertainty caused by the reversal of circumstances combined to make his lot more difficult. He felt alienated, forsaken, and rejected; he longed for reconciliation, fellowship, and acceptance. For the time being, he had to forge ahead in trust and without wavering.

With Dominion

Man participates in the world he governs: not just a part of that world but all of it, not just the pleasant features but the unpleasant ones, and not only in life but in death. There are many ramifications to this truth, but we will limit our discussion to that of suffering. Pain is part of the world man lives in and rules over.

Job again illustrates this. Suffering had invaded his world and threatened to overwhelm him. He longed for those days when all had seemed so ideal, when his family was gathered about the table, which was groaning under ample provision. He could close his eyes to shut out the view of the ash heap extended discouragingly in all directions. But he could not change the state of affairs. This world with all its unattractive features was all he had to work with. This was the only place for him to exercise his dominion.

In an unpublished source, Alice Naumoff imagines the thoughts going through her cat's mind before and after being burned on an electric range. At first the cat puzzled over why her mistress tried to discourage her from approaching the object. She concluded that Miss Naumoff was simply being arbitrary and did not want her to enjoy the liberties that other pets enjoy. Then, when the animal experienced pain caused by a burn, she decided that her

mistress lacked love. Otherwise, Miss Naumoff would
certainly have kept the suffering from her. The mistress
could not win so far as the cat was concerned, although
she had demonstrated her concern time and again. (Once,
Miss Naumoff climbed out on a precarious fire-escape to
rescue the cat, which was crying for deliverance.)

God is no less solicitous for us than Alice Naumoff for
her cat. He had demonstrated His love at great personal
cost. Isaiah wrote:

> But He was pierced through for our transgressions,
> He was crushed for our iniquities;
> The chastening for our well-being fell upon Him,
> And by His scourging we are healed (53:5).

The love of God ought not to be in doubt. And neither
should we question whether He is prepared to embrace
suffering as a condition for redeeming lost mankind.

At Calvary, God internalized pain. There He suffered
on our behalf. He was pierced, crushed, chastened, and
scourged to accomplish His redemptive purpose.

We take our clue for internalizing pain from God. Kazah
Kitamori writes, "Our pain defeats us, and we fear
it . . . because we regard it as an inevitable disaster falling
upon us from *outside* us. As long as we try to escape it, we
cannot resolve it. . . . We can strengthen ourselves when
we earnestly seek and desire pain to be part of our nature."[7] The term *desire* may be misleading in this context.
The author means that we must be prepared to accept
suffering and search for creative ways of handling it. So
long as we reject it, there can be no honest appraisal of life
and no solution to the problems it introduces.

For instance, an English girl, named Ursula, was troubled during her youth by the effects of the industrial
revolution on the one hand and tension between a reli-
giously mystic father and pragmatic mother on the other.

Sunday became disjointed from the remainder of the
week for her. Ursula turned passionately to Sunday and
the sense of security it gave her against the undesirable
features of a large family, an uncertain time, and her
incompatible parents.

She also liked to think of Jesus so long as He did not
become too human. The idea of Jesus having been
crucified was especially repulsive to her.

As Ursula passed over into womanhood, the reality of
the workday world crashed in on her awareness, and "the
religion which had been another world for her, a glorious
sort of play-world, where she lived . . . became a tale, a
myth, an illusion, which, however much one might assert
it to be true as historical fact, one knew was not true—at
least, for this present-day life of ours."[8]

The fantasy world that Ursula had created did not include a true picture of Jesus either; she would imagine
Him walking beneath the trees bidding her walk on the
sea, or breaking bread into five thousand portions, but
suffering was absent. She wanted no consciousness of the
pain of travail, toil, or testing from the now distorted past.
Jesus had remained unrealistically remote, like the white
moon at sunset. Sometimes when the full moon would
rise blood-red over the horizon, she would be terrified
with the recollection that Jesus had suffered the pain of
death.

It is not surprising that Ursula had difficulty in pulling
her life together. She was living in two worlds, neither
being real because they were partial. She had Jesus in the
one and pain in the other, as vividly illustrated when she
was slapped in the face by her sister Theresa. Ursula, in a
mood of piety, silently presented the other side of her
face to the exasperated sister who accommodated with a
more vicious blow. Ursula retreated, stoic without but

boiling within, to await the next argument and to retaliate with a slap calculated to behead her sister.

Jesus and the brutal slap exist not in separate worlds but in the same one. God was pleased to bruise Him (Isa. 53:10), internalizing the suffering, ministering to our pain out of His pain. And Christ calls man not to a fantasy world where pain is the problem, but to a faith world where it can be the occasion for God's blessing. And thus we exercise our dominion over the world.

The resolute figure of Job, for all of his shortcomings, reminds us of how *all* things may work together for our good. All situations can be opportunities for us to foster a deeper communion with the Almighty, minister to and be ministered to by others, and accept our responsibility for the world about us. Those unenviable situations are not only included but may be the better instances for grasping the true significance of life and making progress in our spiritual pilgrimage. Here the superficialities of life are stripped away so that we may get down to the core issues. Here we may discover a vital relationship with God and others and a responsible role over creation. Without such a discovery, we miss the point of life; with it, we will be the richer for our experience. Job reminds us that we can learn to worship and serve even from the ash heap.

Questions for Study and Discussion

1. We are inclined to welcome favorable circumstances and escape by any means the severe trials of life. How may this prove to be our undoing? What theoretical considerations might help us to a more balanced approach to life? What practical steps would help us implement our concern?

2. We considered the nature of man in connection with God and one another. Discuss some of the ideas presented. Weigh the merit of the description of man as to his essential nature.

3. Jesus taught that we should love the Lord our God with all our heart, and with all our soul, and with all our mind and love our neighbor as ourselves (Matt. 2:37, 39). How does this injunction correspond to the discussion of man in relationship to God and others and his dominion over the earth?

4. Job lamented the fact that he had ever been born (3:3, 11). Is it impious to think that way? Why or why not?

5. Kazah Kitamori based his comments on the conviction that the pain of God provides the key to understanding the nature of life. Do you agree with his estimation? If not, do you have a better alternative?

6. Discuss Ursula's dilemma. Have you known of similar instances? What conclusions can you draw after reflecting on such fantasying?

3

Living with Ambiguity

Goal: To welcome ambiguity, God's revelation notwithstanding, as an essential part of life.

Behold, how happy
is the man whom God reproves;
so do not despise the discipline of
the Almighty (Job 5:17).

Among Job's friends Eliphaz was the first to speak. He offered a solution to the patriarch's dilemma. According to Eliphaz, Job had grown callous in the midst of riches and allowed unrighteousness to creep into his life. The misfortune befalling him was God's judgment, a warning to mend his ways. Job could either turn from his sin and be restored to divine favor or persist in his evil and anticipate the continuing heavy hand of God.

Job asked for a bill of particulars. What sins had he committed? Where had he gone wrong? "Teach me, and I will be silent; and show me how I have erred" (6:24). It seems as if Eliphaz had dismissed the ambiguity of the situation too easily. His simplistic explanation allows no alternative, no uncertainty, and not even some qualification.

The Issue

Isaiah extolled the exalted ways of God,

For as the heavens are higher than the earth,
So are My ways higher than your ways,
And My thoughts than your thoughts (Isa. 55:9).

I have sat near the crest of Mount Zion, as the cool night breeze swept over the Hinnon Valley below, and studied the sky. The stars seemed close and yet far away. The air was so clear and the elevation so ideal for observation that I wanted to reach out and pluck myself a star. On the other hand, I was reminded of the great expanse between the heavens and myself. With all of modern technology, we cannot begin to bridge the yawning, dark night that separates man from the distant stars above.

Isaiah explains that although God's word may be published abroad, His ways transcend our own. Like the stars hanging in the firmament above, so close and yet so far away, God reveals His good intentions but obscures their precise workings.

Eliphaz allowed no place for ambiguity in his scheme of things. His discourse was "a forceful poetic statement" to the effect "that God rules the universe in evenhanded justice, and that the sufferings which befall the lot of human kind are retribution for sin. Foolish is the man who thinks, because of temporary prosperity, that he is especially favored and can therefore begin to tamper with the principles of righteousness."[1] Eliphaz's message was at best a partial truth, but when brandished over the tormented Job, it became a vicious cudgel.

Eliphaz and Job drew from the same revelation but arrived at different conclusions. Eliphaz derived a precise formula to explain Job's distress; Job puzzled over the meaning of the turn of events. How do we account for the difference between the two? For an answer, we will have to retrace their steps, beginning with what they held in common and seeing how they eventually parted ways. Such a venture will also give us an opportunity to see how *we* may constructively deal with life's ambiguities.

Point of Departure

The Hebrews were a religious people living among religious neighbors. The Gentiles had "gods for every occasion, and to suit each personal or societal preference; there were clan gods, which protected the family name; there were national gods, which advanced the cause of an emerging people or protected those whose former glory was passing; there were occupational gods, which insured good harvests or healthy issues; there were vengeful gods, which could be induced to hamper one's enemy."[2] The gentile gods behaved little better and sometimes worse than those who worshiped them. These heathen deities defended the vested interests of those in power and at the expense of the masses; they waged war and justified every sort of inhumanity; they were susceptible to bribe; they envied, lusted, caroused, and strove among themselves and with man. Granting the gentile idols their nobler moments, their behavior offended the Hebrews' moral sensitivity.

Neither Eliphaz nor Job supported the heathen pantheon. The myriad of pagan deities were repugnant to them. Thus when Eliphaz emphasized that "God rules the universe in evenhanded justice," he and Job were in agreement. Unlike the permissively religious Gentiles about them, both men acknowledged a God sovereign over the affairs of men. Both likewise accepted the fact that the Almighty holds man strictly accountable for his behavior and that to violate the will of God is to invite retribution.

Now that we have sharpened the focus on this view held in common by contrasting it to the paganism of the time, we may analyze it further. Both Eliphaz and Job believed God to be the living Creator, sovereign over His creation, and thoroughly just in His administration. He alone lives. He alone demonstrates personal qualities, the ability to perceive, evaluate, and act. Other claimants were deaf, dumb, and inactive.

God also rules. Maltbie Babcock reminds us that

> This is my Father's world,
> O let me ne'er forget
> That though the wrong seems oft so strong,
> God is the Ruler yet ("This Is My Father's World").

We ought to tread lightly on this earth for it belongs to the Almighty.

However, man is not a pawn in life's chess game. It is helpful to think of God's sovereignty as resoluteness, meaning that He "presses without exception or respite toward the fulfillment of his holy purpose. . . . We might say that God is leaning on the course of events, steering them toward the eventful climax."[3] He does not preclude man's initiative but takes it into account in achieving His gracious purposes.

God likewise rules justly. The Hebrews knew much

injustice at the hands of their own kings as well as from invading monarchs. Even the better rulers were capable of despicable acts, as in David's affair with Bathsheba, and sometimes an evil tyrant seemed driven by sadistic tendencies. God's rule stood in contrast to all the rest as perfect justice.

The administration of justice has two sides, the one to comfort the afflicted and the other to afflict those comfortable in their sin. If the faith of Eliphaz and Job seems a bit too severe, we are probably looking at only one side of the issue. God's justice promises consolation as well as retribution.

Eliphaz and Job are agreed in the justice of God that declares a man foolish who thinks, because of temporary prosperity, that he is especially favored and can therefore begin to tamper with the principles of righteousness. They believe that God is, rules, and rules justly. But somewhere between this point of departure and the application of that conviction to Job's situation, there comes a parting of the ways. How did this separation come about and what significance does it hold for us?

Eliphaz's Charge

Eliphaz concluded that Job had sinned, thus bringing down God's judgment upon him. He did not have the advantage of reading the preface to the account of Job (the conversation between Satan and God) any more than we have the explanation for experiences we go through. God withholds His own prefaces and conclusions, a solemn fact to bear in mind.

"Show me how I have sinned," Job demands. The cleavage between the two men begins to show. Eliphaz assumes that it is self-evident that Job has erred, thereby inviting God's reprisal; Job cannot settle for such a con-

clusion without some accounting of the facts. Eliphaz
takes a simple correlation between sin and suffering; Job
recognizes ambiguity in life.

You have no doubt heard someone ask: "Why did God
allow this to happen to me? What have I done to suffer
so?" Probably nothing, in the specific sense in which he
puts the question. You cannot point to a time last month
when he pulled a shady business deal as the reason for
contracting cancer. Oh, in the larger sense, sin correlates
to suffering. Had we marshaled all of our energies on a
campaign against cancer, we might have it under control.
And had we not dissipated our energies on less critical
concerns, there would certainly be a higher rate of recov-
ery. But there is no simple correlation between sin and
suffering as Eliphaz seems to feel.

Our sin is but one of a number of factors that influences
our state of being. Take the case of one who drinks to
excess. We know this harms his body, but we do not know
how rugged his condition was in the first place. He may
show early symptoms of his imbibing and die at an early
age. Or he may continue to live a long and vigorous life. It
depends on his ability to resist the bad effects of his
indulgence. We must live with ambiguity.

Good and evil also tend to have a delayed action, show-
ing up in our children and their children after them.
There is truth to the adage that "I got my disposition from
my grandparents." We continue to reap the good and evil
of prior generations. But here also we must struggle with
ambiguity.

We may likewise suffer for righteousness. This fallen
world is no friend to the righteous. They may suffer for
breaking step with the world, and the bystander may
mistake their suffering for divine retribution. There is
ambiguity here as well.

Learning to live with ambiguity does not mean assuming a passive roll. Quite the reverse! It helps us ask the hard questions, even though the answers come with difficulty. It presses us toward responsible action, even though we must move with care. The alternative is far less inviting, because it writes off suffering as simply the result of sin—not any particular sin but sin in general. There is nothing to get at and correct. Only a meaningless generality remains.

Job was right to ask for specifics, to try to get at the problem, to press beyond clichés to the hard realities. His answers came slowly, painfully, reluctantly, but with good results in the end. We can do no better, for ambiguity blurs the ways of life.

Eliphaz's Solution

Eliphaz "offered Job the easy way of submission. He need not acknowledge some specific sin but simply agree that his afflictions are the result of the general sinfulness of men."[4] Eliphaz's solution matches his charge in its generality and emptiness. It tries to say everything and ends up saying nothing specific.

William Peck describes a clinical case that illustrates the problem created by Eliphaz's demand that Job yield. An attractive eighteen-year-old girl was admitted to a private hospital outside Philadelphia. A rather perfunctory smile, coupled with natural beauty, drew one's attention from her intense gaze. Polite and disarmingly coherent, she admitted to an attempt at suicide. Her statement, "Religion should help me, but it doesn't,"[6] indicated the depth of her despair.

The therapist traced the girl's problem back to a conflict between the feeling of rejection and demand for

obedience. One particular incident stood out from among
the rest. At the age of five, she was sent off to relatives for
six weeks, until her brother was born. She developed
during this time a fear of leaving home, which persisted
during childhood and was often accompanied by nausea
and vomiting. Her parents reminded her on these occasions of the obedience she owed them as her parents. And
they rested their case on the biblical injunction, "Children, obey your parents in the Lord, for this is right"
(Eph. 6:1).

The girl was required to obey but felt in the process that
she was being rejected by those she most cared for. Job
likewise heard Eliphaz urge him to submit, but he too felt
the desperation of being forsaken. And while the patriarch does not presume to take his own life, he admits:
"Would that God were willing to crush me; that He would
loose His hand and cut me off!" (6:9).

Eliphaz's solution, like his charge, lacks the necessary
ambiguity to make it credible. The demand to submit
leaves too many things unresolved. It overlooks the deep
anguish of a young child forced to leave the security of her
home, and it disregards the agony of soul built up in a man
who has seen everything in life snatched from his grasp.

In spite of the fallacy of such an approach, religious
people repeatedly fall back on Eliphaz's counsel. I recall
a blind person who had made an excellent adjustment to
his handicap. He regularly surpassed sighted people in
both his physical and mental accomplishments, and he
had developed a most winsome spirituality. However,
some zealous but misled people encouraged him to believe that his blindness would be cured simply if he
submitted to God. "Yield to Him," they urged, and he
attempted to comply. Not only did he fail to regain his
sight, but he lost his quiet confidence as well. His coun-

selors attributed the failure first to God testing his faith, and thereafter to the blind man's lack of trust. They eventually left him alone, another victim of Eliphaz's remedy.

True humility is a virtue, but what often passes for it—an appeal to indiscrimination, thoughtless compliance, or credulity—is not real faith. Proper conclusions are seldom easy to come by, even when we have the appropriate information to consider. They have to be worked with, worked on, and worked out. The appeal for submission is at best a consideration and at worst, a serious detriment.

We must learn to live with tentative, problematic solutions. A good decision today makes for an even better one tomorrow. We can trust God for the light we lack and use what He has provided. We can be confident without being presumptive. And what we gain in the process of deliberation may be more significant than the conclusion itself.

Eliphaz's God

Eliphaz had God neatly packaged. He knew precisely how the Almighty was operating with Job, or so he supposed. John Hick muses, "It may be that God fulfils many different intentions at once and that innumerable strands of the divine activity intersect in the universe in which we live."[6] If that is so, man thinks of life in an incredibly parochial fashion when he imagines that all he sees around him exists only for his personal benefit. God cannot be boxed in. We simply do not know that much about what He has planned for us.

An analogy from human relationships may keep us from falling into Eliphaz's trap. How predictable are the persons we know best? We say that we know how they will respond, only to be thoroughly mistaken. The trained analyst is the first to admit his diagnostic limitations, as if to say that the more we know of others, the less can actually be known.

If we are so limited in our understanding of others, ought we to think that God works in a simpler fashion? A god without hiddenness would not be the God of Scripture. For all of His revelation and because of it, God, from our limited perspectives, remains obscure, mysterious, and unmanageable.

We do well to allow God the prerogative of transcendence and to accept the ambiguity that results. One God is enough; we do not have to know everything about everything. God has revealed what is essential for our well-being, and we can trust Him for the rest.

Eliphaz

We come at last to Eliphaz himself. We have considered his charge, solution, and view of God, but what of the individual? And more particularly, how ought we to see him in relationship to Job?

Psychologist James Dolby points out our need of "at least one trusted person to whom we can confess our shortcomings, tell about our joys, and doubts, our feelings, and all our deep thoughts."[7] In other words, we need a friend. We need someone who will take the time to listen, share, and be thoroughly supportive. Without such a person, life becomes virtually unbearable.

Eiiphaz qualified more as a lecturer than a friend. He proceeded to censure Job. As if Job did not have it bad enough, he had to put up with Eliphaz's incriminations. Eliphaz waved his finger under Job's nose instead of putting his arm around his shoulders in consolation.

One wonders about Eliphaz's peculiar insensitivity. Perhaps Job's calamity worried him about his own precarious situation. If disaster could so quickly befall Job, might he be next in line? Eliphaz's main concern may have been to demonstrate his virtue before the Almighty rather than to assist Job.

This much is certain: Eliphaz demonstrates little interest in Job as a person. He wants to convince the man of his interpretation, but has little patience with the patriarch's complaints. He forces Job's situation to fit a theory, but cares little for the peculiar circumstances of the case. He argues as a man possessed with an idea, but lacks the compassion for feeling the distress of his associate. He talks on and on while Job suffers alone.

Some years ago a young lady confided in me that she felt that much of her difficulty was caused by a poor relationship with her parents. When I asked her whether she was able to talk with her parents about the problems she sensed she responded, "They talk at me, but never with me." We get the impression that Eliphaz was talking *at* Job rather than *with* him. He saw the patriarch as a problem to be overcome instead of a person to be helped.

Eliphaz wanted to keep lines carefully drawn, the sinner in one place and the saint in the other. He wanted to rule out all those gray areas that confuse the picture. But life seldom provides such sharp focus.

Job saw life for what it is, a place where situations are difficult to diagnose, solutions are problematic, God's working is mysterious, and people are a mixture of good and bad. Job accepted ambiguity in faith that God was somehow at work. In the end he was not disappointed.

Questions for Study and Discussion

1. Review Eliphaz's comments to Job (chapters 4–5, 15, 22). Compare your impressions of him with the author's remarks.

2. Do you agree with the thesis that to live in the real world we must be prepared to live with ambiguity? Does this mean that we can never be genuinely confident of God's will in some matter or another?

3. Scripture reads that "he who conceals his transgressions will not prosper, but he who confesses and forsakes them will find compassion" (Prov. 28:13). How do Job's and Eliphaz's interpretations of the thought conveyed by this verse differ? How do you account for the contrast?

4. How do you understand James's injunction "Submit therefore to God" (James 4:7)? How may Eliphaz have misappropriated the necessity of submission? Is there some indication that Job better grasped what is involved in yielding to God's will?

5. J. B. Phillips wrote a popular book entitled *Your God Is Too Small*. Are there indications that Eliphaz was suffering from this problem? When is our God too small? How can we enlarge our perceptions of the Almighty?

4

Learning from Tradition

Goal: To draw upon
the legacy of the past
without becoming enslaved
to it.

Please inquire of
past generations, and
consider the things searched out by
their fathers. For we are only
of yesterday and know nothing,
because our days on earth are
as a shadow (Job 8:8–9).

Eliphaz stepped back to let Bildad pick up the discussion with Job. "Please inquire of past generations," he urged the patriarch. Let revered tradition instruct us in its way. "For we are only of yesterday and know nothing," a mere shadow of the former substance. We can only draw superficial conclusions from fleeting impressions. Tradition remains the more trustworthy guide.

Job, however, wants the matter updated. History never repeats itself in precisely the same form, so we cannot expect tradition to apply precisely to the present. There must be an application made, and that application is seldom obvious from the outset.

These two points of view stand in contrast to each other. Bildad seems to see the past as a prized observation post from which we easily slip and to which we must climb back. Job appears to think of the past as a stepping-stone to a richer, fuller life in the present. It is Job's sage perspective that we want to investigate as we sort it out from Bildad's counterargument.

Appeal to Loyalty

"We in this age know nothing, he [Bildad] says, but the fathers of old will teach us. He sets himself up as the champion of the wisdom of the ages, whereas Job is the rebel against all true wisdom."[1] Bildad appeals first to Job on the basis of loyalty. As a subject serves his country or a son honors his father, so Job should heed the sage counsel of the past. Any failure to do so brands him as an unappreciative revolutionary.

Bildad's rationale clouds the issue. The past deserves our consideration but not solely or exactly for the reason he sets forth. There are two reasons that come to the fore: history affects us in any case and it also suggests the range of options available to us. These appear to be the considerations that guide Job's response to Bildad's plea for his uncritical loyalty to the past.

To ignore the past would be detrimental. Our time in history resembles the most recent chapter in a long book. To commence reading with the present would be to miss all that led up to it and result in a failure to see how each person's life intertwines with and derives meaning from the rest. Job seems to have appreciated this fact.

He also recognized that we may learn from past successes and failures. Only those who take the past seriously can hope to benefit from the trails others have blazed or escape the pitfalls into which others have fallen. Job treats the past as a prized legacy from which to draw rather than a fixed rule from which we dare not stray.

Job might be misunderstood at this point. I recall a young man who purposely discarded all biblical commentary to get "a fresh approach to Scripture." He groped for his way and stumbled around in the process, while ignoring the available help. Job advocates no such categorical rejection of tradition but a sensitive and sensible use of it.

But tradition includes the bad as well as the good, the trivial as well as the crucial. We have to sort out the different elements. Bildad gives the impression that Job must respect tradition in all of its connections with equal fervor. Such a conclusion is not only wrong but tragic.

Take the case of a man raised in a very religious home who eventually rejected the faith of his parents. His religious tradition had been presented to him as a package deal—accept everything or nothing at all. Each conviction seemed of equal significance, whether concerning the person of Christ or some incidental feature of a preferred lifestyle. Thus having been denied the possibility of modifying his religious tradition at some point or another as seemed proper, he surrendered it all with one sweeping capitulation.

Job offers the wiser course of action. He asks that we appreciate the past for what it has to offer, by way of understanding ourselves and the options life affords us.

He suggests that we build upon the past and not be satisfied with observing what others have built.

Appeal to Obligation

Bildad implies another reason for Job to keep in touch with tradition. He should do so not only because a legacy had been left to him, but also because he had the responsibility of passing this legacy on to others. Paul seemed to have this in mind when he wrote to Timothy, "And the things which you have heard from me in the presence of many witnesses, these entrust to faithful men, who will be able to teach others also" (II Tim. 2:2). What the youthful preacher had received, he was to dispense to others, who would in turn share it with still a larger audience.

Bildad is correct to a point. We err in thinking that tradition pertains to us alone and not to subsequent generations as well. We are obligated to cherish and pass on the legacy we have received.

But how can we best fulfill our responsibility for tradition? Hugh Hopkins observes that "Character is not formed in the hectic rush of escapism. . . . Psychologically it is fatal. Spiritually it is the admission of failure."[2] We succeed not by repeating word for word what someone has said but by living out that sage counsel in a new set of circumstances.

Bildad seems to have a static concept of tradition. One must pass on with care what he received without allowing it to interact with life at any juncture. Or, like the unprofitable servant in Jesus' story, he must guard what has been given him rather than put it to good use (Matt. 25:24–25). Hopkins suggests that such an approach is psychologically fatal and spiritually an admission of failure. In the latter connection, it is clear that Jesus taught likewise.

Job clearly anticipates a more dynamic use of tradition. He expects life to continue, drawing upon the past but qualifying it as appropriate. Tradition appears to him as an on-going experience of appreciating and interpreting more fully the truth he has received.

We all know of persons who have difficulty assuming Job's dynamic stance toward tradition. There comes to mind a woman who made a practice of circumventing unpleasant duties until it became impossible for her to face reality. She took shelter in her marriage, children, home, and recreation so as to ignore the harsher aspects of life. When these could no longer shield her, she broke under the onrush of concerns she could no longer disregard. Her religious faith had also served as an opiate. It helped her escape the difficult circumstances of life rather than cope with them. Her view of tradition resembled that of Bildad.

Job reminds us that we have an appointment with God in life's forum. There He promises to meet us: where people gather, talk, shove, and hurt. We ought not to expect to find Him in some hidden place, away from where humanity surges.

The Almighty wants us to pick up the cup of life and drink deeply. There is bitterness as well as sweetness, and when life becomes so difficult that we cry out with Jesus, "If it is possible, let this cup pass from me," we are quick to add, "yet not as I will, but as Thou wilt" (Matt. 26:39). We may taste bitterness, but we will not have failed to drink as God bids us.

We are certainly encouraged to pass on the legacy of the past, but we should do so by living it out in the present. Then we speak from conviction forged in the dynamic interplay of tradition with life. Then we speak on our own behalf and not simply report what others have said.

Appeal to God

Under Bildad's prodding, the discussion turns finally to the subject of eternity. Suffering is but the prelude to death, and after death, what is there to be considered?

After death, what then? This is an arresting thought. We tend to think of this life, its rewards and demands, and interpret suffering in the context of three score and ten years. We wonder how pain may frustrate or further the good life here and now in the brief span of years allotted to us. But Job is not content to stop there. After death, what then?

Job had witnessed death and talked about it. But perhaps for the first time, under Bildad's bombardment, he accepted the reality of death for himself. He faced the fact of death. Although man has increased his domination over nature and has extended his powers, all ends abruptly for him. He cannot cheat death of its prize, no matter how hard he tries. After his life has held out so much promise, his physical existence finally leads to defeat.

Failure awaits us and nothingness as well. Paul Tillich says that man "came from nothing, and he returns to nothing."[3] We fashion an existence for ourselves, drawing upon our legacy for meaning. We struggle to sustain this frail and passing episode in history only to slip back into the dust from which we came. We are and then are no longer. Even the memories that try to recall us cannot recover life. There seems to be nothing left.

Tolstoy tells the story of an elderly man conspicuous for his refusal to cross himself upon hearing the bells of a nearby church.

"Why do you not pray?" he was asked.

"Who is one to pray to?" came the answer.

"To whom? To God, of course," was the withering rejoinder.

"And you just show me where He is—this God?" invited the unrepentant man.

Seeing that the person would not be shamed, his critic responded, "Where? In heaven of course."

The aroused person pressed the issue, "And have you been up there?"

"Whether I've been or not," objected the other, "every one knows that one must pray to God. It's clear you are not a Christian, but a hole-worshiper.You pray to a hole."

Tolstoy interprets the *hole-worshiper's* creed as accepting no name but that of man, and no belief but the confidence derived from man.[4]

Job had something in common with both men of Tolstoy's story, the traditional believer and the humanist. Along with the former Job confessed "And as for me, I know that my Redeemer lives, and at the last He will take His stand on the earth. Even after my skin is flayed, yet without my flesh I shall see God" (19:25–26). After death, God would be there. After nothingness, God would be there. After the hole, heaven awaits.

"In a moment of intuitive insight," William Ward speculates, "Job knows that after his death he will plead his case before God himself and God will openly defend and justify him."[5] Bildad and Job had argued the respective merits of their cases, sometimes concurring but more often disagreeing. However, when each would breathe his last, when every weighty consideration would be vanished, then God alone would greet the silence. Either our hope must be in the Almighty or nothing.

It may seem for the time being that we can get along

well enough without God, but only for now and only in our imagination. Tolstoy's "hole" testifies to impending death but awakens us to the reality of life. Either God sustains us now and through a cruel interruption called death, or our hope and life are in vain. Such seems to be the realization that Job comes to, perhaps not a totally new one for him but one that breaks upon him with renewed force.

The patriarch also had something in common with the hole-worshiper, which distinguished him from Bildad. The hole-worshiper believed in what he saw. If he observed man, he believed in him. He took the world and his experience with life seriously. Job also took his present circumstance seriously; he did not write it off with some religious platitude.

The traditionalist, like Bildad or the pious man in Tolstoy's story, runs the danger of substituting some religious sentiment for life itself. The reassuring sound of a church bell, the crossing of oneself by way of response, or the reciting of familiar religious traditions can easily short-circuit living. They trivialize life's more profound moments, rush answers before we have felt the strength of the questions, speak so loudly that we cannot hear a word life is trying to say to us.

Job resisted the religious dodge to take the full blow of his dilemma. In this respect, he was like the hole-worshiper. But here the similarity ceased, for Job caught a vision of what transcended his immediate situation. He saw God in his future, and the present was transformed for him.

Options Contrasted

Marc Oraison makes an astute observation: "Since my encounter with someone else is . . . always a focus of pain, how much more is this true of our relationship with Someone Else with whom we have nothing in common at all."[6] Tradition may become a defense mechanism that shields us not only from one another but from communion with God. Bildad's accent on tradition obscured his vision of God.

"Look over your shoulder," Bildad urged. Out of a feeling of appreciation, look back; out of a sense of responsibility for future generations, look back; out of the realization of your own limitations, look back. The Savior awaits you back there. Bildad's varied appeals to loyalty, obligation, and finitude now seem more defensive than when we first heard them. They appear to be shallow and protective—less calculated to be of real help to Job in his despair.

By contrast, the patriarch's interest remained fixed on the present, not excluding the past but demanding to know its relevance. Abraham Heschel urges that our "inquiry must proceed both by delving into the consciousness of man as well as by delving into the teachings and attitudes of the religious tradition."[7] Bildad demands a decision for the past at the expense of the present, whereas Heschel and Job concur in relating the two.

Only when we see the importance of former times for our on-going experience can it be said that we have genuinely learned from tradition. Then we can see how tradition shapes our life, passes on the wisdom of the past, captures the wonder of living, and invites us to worship. We can also sense the importance of meeting God where we are by drawing upon the past to assist us and sharing the benefits gained through our experience.

For all of Bildad's talk about God, he seems unfamiliar with the Almighty. You get the feeling that if he had lived back with the fathers he delights to discuss, he would not have shared in their experiences. For Job things were different. Troubled though he was, the patriarch reaches out for the Almighty, staying in there with life, and searching for its meaning.

It should not surprise us that men like Bildad fashion religious mechanisms to postpone such fateful meetings with God. It should encourage us to see Job push ahead in spite of the painful prospect of such an encounter. With religious tradition Bildad shielded himself from a face to face confrontation with God. But Job demanded an audience with God. When tradition introduces us to the Almighty, we owe it our gratitude. Tradition is a good teacher and faithful guide. But our faith must not end with this.

Questions for Study and Discussion

1. Thomas Carlyle wrote, "No truth or goodness realized by man ever dies, or can die; but is all still here, and, recognized or not, lives and works through endless changes" (*Sir Walter Scott*). What does this suggest for those who would learn from the past?

2. Review Bildad's discourses (chapters 8, 18, 25). What conclusions do you draw concerning his perspective on life in general, and Job's situation in particular? How do they compare with the author's appraisal?

3. What was misleading in Bildad's appeals to loyalty, duty, and devotion to God? Restate these admonitions without falling into Bildad's error.

4. Would you agree that Job had something in common with both men in Leo Tolstoy's account of their response to the ringing of a church bell? What are the respective dangers of taking one point of view or the other? What are the strengths of each of the men's perspectives?

5. Compare Bildad to Eliphaz. How do their points of view seem to agree or disagree? Does one of them seem nearer to

Job's position than the other? Or, are their views equally rep-
rehensible?

6. It is sometimes said that we need all kinds of persons.
Ought we to expect substantial differences in those we meet
and can this work to our advantage? If so, how? If not, why not?

Countering Prejudice

Goal: To correct the bias that often passes for an expression of piety.

How often is the lamp
of the wicked put out, or their
calamity fall on them? Does God
apportion destruction in His anger?
Are they as straw before the
wind, and like chaff
which the storm carries
away? (Job 21:17–18).

Next, Zophar bursts into the discussion with Job. Lacking Eliphaz's more reasoned approach or Bildad's historical preference, Zophar seems determined to make up for these by a bombastic offense. He advances with a flurry of verbal blows, as if thinking that forcefulness will succeed where finesse had failed.

Seen through the eyes of Job, the new speaker combines prejudice with sophistry, a warped view of things coupled with a deliberate misrepresentation of the facts. One could imagine from the patriarch's response how Zophar may have appeared to him. He appears as standing haughtily erect, body tense, and with grim countenance. His mind is made up, and he sees his task as that of convincing obstinate Job.

About Prejudice

Zophar brashly announced that God had exacted less from Job than his guilt deserved (11:6) and followed up this presumptive charge with a clear distortion of the patriarch's behavior (20:18–21). His prejudice (reaching a decision before weighing the facts) drips with each succeeding comment. The saying goes, "My mind is made up; do not confuse me with the facts." This seems to have been Zophar's approach.

Job reflected a more open attitude, a willingness to examine alternatives and reappraise previously held opinions. But he must have compelling evidence to change his mind.

Zophar treats Job as though he were thoroughly ignorant of God's ways. He taunts the patriarch, "Can you discover the depths of God? Can you discover the limits of the Almighty?" (11:7).

Zophar also charges the patriarch as being reprobate. He has sinned even more grievously than God's punishment would imply. Job's protest of innocence only confirms his guilt.

Thus prejudice handles opposition: either as an instance of ignorance or evil intent. It asserts itself in the face of contradiction, as if to overwhelm all else by its uncompromising insistence.

How are we to press beyond prejudice? How are we to struggle from Zophar's position to that of Job? We must first recognize that there are good reasons why people see things differently. Life resembles a circle of people surveying an intricate painting. One sees one thing and another, something else, and the whole is interpreted in terms of what aspect impressed the viewer most.

We all err in some measure as a result. We give more importance to one consideration than we should and less importance to another than appropriate. And we skew life accordingly.

But that is not to say that we have failed to see anything of life, even though from a distorted perspective. There are partial truths waiting to be refined, corrected, added to, and elaborated. No person has a monopoly in understanding.

Then are all views equally valid? Not in the least. Some people have a better grasp on reality than others because they see more of the picture or have it in better focus. What matters is how large a circle we allow—whether it takes into consideration all the pertinent facts or merely some of them. Zophar's circle was pathetically small, whereas Job attempted to expand his to gain a true assessment of the situation.

Sometimes we have all the needed data but simply do not know how to properly tie it together. The instructor asks a question, only to be met with an uneasy silence from his students. "You have the information necessary to answer my question," he exhorts them, and indeed they have, if they can relate one thing to another.

We press beyond prejudice by recognizing the validity in perspectives other than our own and reaching for a more complete and better focused perspective as a result. Thus we leave Zophar's side to join with the sage in his quest for understanding. We open our minds to truth wherever it may be discovered, for genuine truth must be God's truth as well.

To escape from prejudice, we must also contend with deep-rooted feelings. As children we have been relatively indiscriminate in the way we associated our feelings (good or bad) with some experience or another. We failed to appreciate that what seemed pleasant on a given occasion was due to a qualification rather than the thing itself. And we zealously guarded the experience from any reflection that might break the cherished pattern. We even built an elaborate defense system by rationalizing our behavior on the basis of plausible but invalid considerations.

We cannot ignore such emotions, but we need not pamper them. There are more rewarding experiences waiting for those who will leave their infantile perceptions behind for a mature adult life. But it means that we must let go of the one to grasp hold of the other.

The mature person accepts that he should do certain things and refrain from others. It is not enough to say, "I feel like it" or "I do not feel like it." Such an appeal to emotion disallows the sifting of evidence and leaves us bogged down in bias.

The prejudiced person has a predictable behavior. He acts according to a prescribed role. There is little adaptation to others and even less creativity of his own.

The pattern of prejudice characteristically is set in the home. It develops when the emphasis is placed on reciprocal services rather than relationships. It is fostered when insufficient time is taken to explain the rationale for the way we behave, and we demand instead unquestioning compliance and enforce conformity by reward and punishment.

Consider the example of a mother whose child keeps interrupting an important telephone conversation. She can insist that the child wait a few minutes, and after she hangs up the phone she will do her best to help him and explain why it was important to conclude the telephone conversation. Solid relationships are forged in such a fashion.

But if an irate mother simply screams at the child to shut up and makes no effort to explain her reason for doing so, the child may learn something about role playing but little concerning relationship. Multiply such instances many times and one can expect to reap prejudice.

It is never too late to weaken the hold that prejudice has on us and begin to build relationships. We begin by recognizing a certain validity to viewpoints other than our own, pressing to refine the insights (theirs and ours), coping with our uncritical feelings, and building bridges to others.

Zophar's approach threatened to destroy any bridges that might have existed between Job and himself. He complains, "Shall a multitude of words go unanswered, and a talkative man be acquitted?" (11:2). Zophar saw the patriarch as boastful and as a scoffer but not a person with unfulfilled needs. There was no possibility for building a relationship, only to play the role of accuser.

We all too easily fall into Zophar's pattern. A man once warned me about the evils of the communist world conspiracy. He became tense as he talked, his eyes peering through slits meant to convey the seriousness of the topic, his voice dropping to an appropriately husky whisper: "They have infiltrated everywhere and we must show them no mercy." Regardless of the validity of his statement, I doubt that he ever knowingly met a Communist. But more pertinent, he could not think of a Communist as a person similar to himself. A person's political philosophy blinded him from discovering *who* he really might be.

Beyond bias is an inviting world where beliefs may be investigated and firmed up, feelings explored and put on sounder bases, and action directed to the service of our fellow man. Life is too rich to be viewed from a narrow, partisan perspective. Conviction, the kind of conviction that takes hold of life, must be cognizant of the whole and convinced of the best. Job would soon leave Zophar behind in his quest for better things.

Subterfuge

"Listen carefully," Job admonishes, as if to make a valiant effort at correcting the fallacy his friends had propounded. Then, singling out one of them (probably Zophar), he anticipates further mockery (21:2–3). Job's sincerity stands in sharp contrast to Zophar's sophistry.

Sophistry derives from the Greek teachers of rhetoric, who traveled about imparting the secrets of convincing speech, making "the worse appear the better cause." They tested their skills in making the impossible seem obvious, and the true appear false. The Sophists practiced not for the love of truth but for the power of persuasion. They enjoyed the ability to manipulate.

What had Job recognized in Zophar's bombastic treatment? Apparently Zophar liked to listen to himself, to sense his capability of expressing ideas and observing their effect on others. His was a game orators sometime play. Job felt the sting of the jibes, but remained unimpressed with the logic. He rejected "as useless sophistry the argument of the misfortunes of the wicked which the friends have monotonously advanced."[1]

"Useless sophistry," the patriarch concludes concerning Zophar's performance, "monotonously advanced." Protagoras comes down through history to us as one of the leading and least to be reproached of the Sophists. Nevertheless, he "felt that moral behavior could be taught much as grammar or arithmetic could. A set of precepts telling you how to act to your own best advantage could be memorized and applied."[2] Without going into such controversial issues as Protagoras's alliance with the rich against the poor and subverting the youth of ancient Greece, we sense that his key to life was how to manipulate others to his own advantage.

Most of us can recall experience with manipulators. For all of their better qualities, they can decide on something they want and do everything in their power to get it.

The manipulator complicates life for others. He is forever interrupting more important things with less significant ones; suppressing your concerns to his; shuffling priorities without consulting those implicated. He is a parasite on humanity, drawing on the energy of others to pamper his own indulgence.

Jesus stands sublime in bold contrast to the manipulator. He said of Himself, "the Son of Man did not come to be served, but to serve, and to give His life a ransom for many" (Matt. 20:28). Joachim Jeremias comments further, "There is no parallel to Jesus sitting down in table-fellowship with publicans and sinners. There is no parallel to the authority with which he dares to address God as *abba*."[3] Although that is true, Jesus also taught His disciples to emulate Him. "You know that the rulers of the Gentiles lord it over them, and their great men exercise authority over them," He observed. "It is not so among you, but whoever wishes to become great among you shall be your servant" (Matt. 20:25–26). Thus the disciple behaves as a son of God and brother to his fellow man.

"In the most elementary terms, being a son meant observing the father's will; being brothers meant sharing in that concern."[4] A faithful son abides by his father's will.

The faithful son of God disciplines himself to live in his Father's world and with his Father's help. He does not permit any other consideration to detract from his obedience to the Almighty. His concern resides not with pleasing himself but in finding acceptance with God. He takes pleasure in living out Jesus' words, "Not as I will, but as Thou wilt."

Only through such resolute obedience can we hope to experience all that God has in store for us. As one travels south from the Judean hill country, through the lowlands, and toward the desert, vegetation becomes less and less evident. Soon you see wilderness stretching in every direction, except for the convergence of river beds. There some enterprising farmer has tapped the last water resources to eke out a slim harvest. In years when the rainfall drops off, this marginal endeavor becomes impossible, and he must retreat to better water supplies. Life resembles that situation. Some people open their lives so minimally to God as to live constantly in danger of drying up. Unfavorable circumstances come along and the little they have experienced wilts before their eyes. Others draw from plentiful wells that resist the changes of climate and bear fruit year after year. The latter are those who experience life as sons of God.

As one has experienced the grace of God, so should he be eager to share with others. Paul observed that "he who sows bountifully shall also reap bountifully. Let each one do just as he has purposed in his heart; not grudgingly or under compulsion; for God loves a cheerful giver" (II Cor. 9:6–7).

The contrast now stands complete. We have the Sophist on the one hand and the son/brother on the other. The one goes after what he wants at the expense of others; the latter seeks what God has to offer for himself and his fellow man. Zophar combines bias and sophistry into a horrible blend of foul medicine, which Job refuses in favor of a more open and rewarding expectation.

To Sum Up

I sometimes wonder about the wisdom of writing concerning things we know so little. My earlier theories on child training proved unrealistic when confronted with the actual situation. They became fewer and less certain with each succeeding child. Perhaps Zophar felt proficient at spinning theories because he had experienced so little of living. He touched life only in an incidental fashion. Prejudice closes the door to life's rewarding nuances, and sophistry slams down the windows, leaving us with the stale air of our make-believe worlds.

Job's response to his associate's prattle is genuinely humorous, "Truly then you are the people, and with you wisdom will die!" (12:2). How somber Zophar must have appeared as he lectured exasperated Job. On he went without letup until the patriarch broke in with his comment. And Job's tortured expression must have eased for the moment at the prospect of the epitaph, "Wisdom Perished with Zophar."

George Buttrick concludes that "modern atheism is suspect because it has so little power to laugh at itself."[5] He may be right. In any case, it does not serve man to be hyper-serious. Why? Because it upsets the cycle of life: celebration and deliberation, deliberation and celebration. Both are biblical admonitions: "Praise the Lord!" (Ps. 147:1, 12, 20) and "Come now, let us reason together" (Isa. 1:18). Job's friends were lacking in celebration as they persisted with deliberation. As a result they brought little light and no joy to what was already a dark situation.

The patriarch's tormentors have many who share their gloomy appraisal of life. C. S. Lewis confessed: "No slightest hint was vouchsafed me that there ever had been or ever would be any connection between God and Joy. If anything, quite the reverse."[6] For all he knew, the total rejection of happiness might have been the cost for following the Lord. It came as a latent surprise to Lewis that the "arrows of joy" shot at him from childhood came from God's bow.

Zophar offered the patriarch prejudice, reinforced by sophistry, resulting in a motionless and mirthless suspension, but Job refused the offer. He had no appetite for ashes but could see that Zophar's alternative would give him no place to plant his feet and face life. The patriarch chose rather to push beyond bias and shun manipulation to appreciate life in its fullness, even when the way appeared painful to travel. He reached out to God and others for companionship, allowed himself the tonic of a little laughter, and took the better way.

William Cowper sums up Job's experience in *Light Shining Out of Darkness:*

> Judge not the Lord by feeble sense,
>   But trust Him for His grace;
> Behind a frowning providence,
>   He hides a smiling face.

To live beyond prejudice and sophistry, we need, by the grace of God, to welcome life in all its complexity, endless variety, and limitless possibilities. Job does well to press ahead for fear that he might miss some good thing that the Almighty holds in store for him.

Questions for Study and Discussion

1. Distinguish prejudice from conviction. How does Zophar illustrate the one and Job the other?

2. Review Zophar's contribution to the discussion (chapters 11, 20). Do you sense any progression in the argument taken by each man in his turn? Is there any indication that Job's associates have softened their opinions as a result of the patriarch's protest or that the reverse has been the case?

3. "Train up a child in the way he should go, even when he is old he will not depart from it" (Prov. 22:6). How may we insure that youth will not fall prey to prejudice? Draw up a series of suggestions for parents to follow.

4. How may sophistry readily grow in the soil of prejudice? Explore this subtle relationship for whatever caution and corrective may be discovered.

5. Jesus said to His disciples, "If any one wishes to come after Me, let him deny himself, and take up his cross, and follow Me" (Matt. 16:24). How might this text bear on the contrast made between Jesus and Protagoras (the son/brother and manipulator)?

6. C. S. Lewis comments that errors normally occur in opposite pairs. In attempting to avoid prejudice, what snare might we fall into?

Cultivating Faith

Goal: To distinguish between faith and credulity, to nourish the one and eliminate the other.

Wait for me a little,
and I will show you that
there is yet more to be said in
God's behalf. I will fetch my
knowledge from afar, and I will
ascribe righteousness
to my Maker (Job 36:2–3).

Two concerns caused Elihu to break his self-imposed silence: Job's persisting claim to innocence and his associates' inability to persuade him otherwise. These competing factors provoked the last of the patriarch's companions to speak out. "Wait for me," he urged Job, "and I will show you that there is yet more to be said in God's behalf."

Elihu also expects to succeed wherein others had failed. Previously, he had restrained himself out of respect for those older than he. He listened as their arguments turned this way and that, only to miss their intended target. How inept his elders appeared as Job countered one thrust after another! Now he elected to take up the task, and asks Job to trust his solution.

The question of credibility enters with Elihu. No one should doubt the necessity of having faith. To negotiate life at all, we must believe in something, somehow. We cannot choose whether to believe, but we must decide among the vast array of possibilities presented for our consideration. Here Job finds himself, as must we all.

Faith

"Faith is considered trust, accepting God's pledge at face value, and acting upon it."[1] Credulity is uncalled-for trust; trust poorly grounded. For example, the Amba tribe believe that certain gods *catch* people to assure that sacrifice will be made to them. They point to fainting and dizziness as the major symptoms of this capture, although visions and trances may also qualify. The disturbances these gods create are meant to gain attention, and only if their victims ignore their desires will more serious measures be taken.[2] Some still hang on to such traditional beliefs, although they find it increasingly difficult to do so. More plausible explanations replace them as former convictions lose their credibility.

These so-called primitive beliefs are not exceptions. We all have believed something that we no longer hold. Some beliefs strain under the weight of contrary evidence until they collapse. Others seem to be refined in the crucible of life until they become strong and durable.

Genuine faith implies an appropriate response on our part. Consider Dietrich Bonhoeffer's statement, "Only he who believes is obedient, and only he who is obedient believes."[3] Whichever way one looks at the subject, reliance and execution belong together. You will find a person who argues that he is trusting in God when that actually is not the case. He runs his business as if the Almighty were unconcerned; he manages his home as if God were excluded; he indulges himself as if the Lord had no wider circle of interest. But those who really believe put their faith into practice.

The reverse is also true: the obedient believe. This is the way it must be since we do not yet see the results for which we hope. When Jesus met the two brothers Simon and Andrew He said to them "Follow Me, and I will make you fishers of men" (Matt. 4:19). They left all in response to His call, and they trusted Jesus for the rest. Eventually they would become fishers of men, but for now they must obey Jesus' directive to follow Him. Their obedience required faith.

Often we get faith and feeling confused. We talk of having *faith* when we mean *feeling*. Bonhoeffer did not say that he who is obedient feels. The obedient soul may or may not experience a profound sense of peace or an overpowering exultation, but he nevertheless trusts. Even if his senses cry out in anguish, he believes. Certainly belief/obedience influences our feelings, but the former logically and experientially precedes the latter. If we have trouble believing, we should obey, and if we stumble in obedience, we should believe. These are alternate doors into the same room.

Elihu demanded that Job place his confidence in him, but the patriarch refused. Faith is too precious a commodity to place it thoughtlessly in another. Think through the credentials offered, listen carefully to the claim made, and if the case warrants it, act boldly. Otherwise, hold back, stay clear, and restrain faith for a better occasion.

Too many people compromise their convictions for expediency. To marry, to keep peace in the family, or to climb higher in the business firm faith is often compromised. To what end? Perhaps with some return, but always with a measurable loss. One young lady agreed to bring up her children in a faith she could not espouse. How bitter that lie became for her, observing silence when she felt compelled to speak, speaking words that stuck in her throat, and all the time agonizing within herself. Job chose the better way, probably more difficult for the moment but much preferred over the long run.

We should pause to inquire how Job's suffering tied into the subject of faith. William Fitch observes that "God uses pain to make us trust Him more."[4] Fitch does not claim that suffering initiates trust. One had better come by faith in more favorable circumstances than expecting adversity to bring it on. Pain has been popularized far too often as a cure for faithlessness. Actually, more often than we would like to think, suffering drives a person deeper into his degradation, despair over coping with life, or an artless effort to bargain with God.

Fitch does suggest that the Almighty uses pain for His purpose. Here we recall the earlier discussion of the complex good, to which repented sin and suffering contribute. Given a teachable spirit, God employs suffering as a means of instruction. In the hour of trial, he demonstrates His own faithfulness and the fickle nature of the idols we are tempted to believe in.

It has been said that "the best thing about sickness is that it forces you to look up." With back pressed against the bed, with eyes fixed upon the ceiling, and mind interrupted from its obsessions with trivia, we sense the meaninglessness of our round of activities. The superficial things we have cherished take flight, leaving us to face our crisis.

Fortunate indeed is the man who discovers the Almighty at such a moment. It can happen as many testify. When all else failed them, they detected the Almighty standing by. They did not relish the experience of suffering as such but counted it a blessing that through this means they found the Lord.

This is not, however, the point of Fitch's observation. He is not thinking of an initial encounter with the Almighty but a deepening of one's experience with Him. He suggests that pain helps us trust God *more* than previously. A steady diet of pain has seldom done anyone much good, but suffering in the midst of experiencing God's providential concern can enrich life. When one has drawn upon God's blessing in the good times, he can hold on to God's grace in the bad ones. And his spiritual life may mature as a result.

Pain drove Job to a solution deeper than that proposed by Elihu. Rabbi Rava illustrated this by his counsel to those afflicted. When stricken, the rabbi suggests that first we scrutinize our past deeds to see if there can be found anything that displeases God. Should nothing be discovered, then consider that we may have shirked some responsibility. If by this time no cause can be singled out, conclude that we are being chastened out of God's love.[5] "For whom the Lord loves He reproves," the rabbi recalls, "even as a father the son in whom he delights" (Prov. 3:12). Whatever the circumstance, whether we can discern what is involved or not, know that God works with us as a concerned parent and accept pain as a gentle corrective. Know this also: pain holds a great potential

when in the hands of the master Teacher and applied to a
highly motivated student.

Elihu stopped much too short with his appeal for Job's
trust. He determined that the patriarch's suffering could
be caused by nothing less than exceptional guilt. He
failed to probe deeper into the possibility that this was an
occasion for learning some of life's most precious truths
and bearing witness of them to others. Faith, in more than
name only, must pick its way through the alternatives
Rabbi Rava elaborates, until it comes to the place of
resting in God's wisdom and mercy.

Certainty

Elihu was as assured of his conclusions as he was incor-
rect in them. Sometimes we fare better for being less
confident.

Where had Elihu's assurance sprung from? From his
youthfulness (32:7–10). Elihu's patience with the older
generation had run out; now he speaks with a confidence
born of hasty consideration.

Elihu's dissatisfaction with the older generation is not
without provocation. Age does not come with a guarantee
of wisdom, as we have seen with Job's associates. But if
that is so, youth qualifies even less. Whereas the older
generation may hide behind established ways, the
younger generation has yet to put the alternatives to a
serious test.

Paul Sherer reports the comments of a college sopho-
more: "I have heard a good many preachers, and read a
good many religious books; now I have made up my mind
that all of it has to go. I must begin for myself, and begin to
scratch."[6] Sherer responds that since such an attitude
would not work in a chemical laboratory, it should not be

thought adequate for religious life. His comment hits the mark. No specialist, let alone a fledgling, approaches his work without giving careful consideration to what others have done in the field. Why should we suppose that this would not apply to the realm of religious faith?

"Pay attention," Elihu demands. "Keep silent, and I will teach you wisdom" (33:31, 33). His youthful candor comes across as brashness, if not utter rudeness. That Job fails to respond is not surprising.

Elihu seems shaken by the patriarch's lack of response and turns for support from others. "Men of understanding will say to me, and a wise man who hears me, 'Job speaks without knowledge, and his words are without wisdom' " (34:34-35). This appeal also seems ill-advised. Who can say what the concensus of others might be? Such generalizations do little to strengthen Elihu's credibility.

One step remains for Elihu. He has argued from the vantage point of youth (not without some merit) and with the assent of others (an important but not final consideration), but turns at last to God to back his feeble play. His eyes sweep the heavens for support, and his hand calls Job's attention to the celestial blackboard. "Elihu begins to draw illustrations of divine majesty and mystery from the gathering of the thick storm cloud, the flash of lightning on the sand dunes and the roll of thunder across the heavens."[7] He sees the gathering clouds as God's proof of his position, lightning cutting across the skies as a divine punctuation for his sentences, the crash of thunder as the Almighty's deep-throated amen to his words.

Elihu's erroneous presumption to speak for God can take either an individual or corporate turn. I recall a person who decided to drop certain responsibilities that he had earlier agreed to fulfill. He claimed that this was God's leading. He urged others to accept his "religious insight." He had assumed a private line to the Almighty, received privileged information as a result, and now had a blanket indulgence for his action.

This deception can overtake an entire group of people as well. Denominational or cultic groups imagine themselves to be a select people who alone know the mind of God and serve His purpose.

One can readily appreciate the appeal for religious certainty. We hear so many conflicting points of view. If someone only would provide us with the final word! Well and good, so long as that last word is God's word. But this is where the rub comes, when persons profess to speak for God without biblical authority to do so.

Elihu dangled his religious certainties before Job, but the patriarch wisely refused to bite. The tempting lure meant to drag him into credulity, to put fiction in place of fact. Job realized that faith must be able to weigh the various alternatives, to discard the false and accept the true, and that the appeal to religious certainty often thrives on man's lack of faith, drawing him to an uncritical commitment and chaining him to an unreflective following. An untroubled faith is not faith at all, because as with Elihu it flies away from the ambiguities of life. Real faith dares to hear the contrary charges, the hard questions, and the persisting difficulties. Like Job it dares to press to a responsible commitment.

Righteousness

Job's claim to innocence especially incensed Elihu. "Do you say," he gasped, that your "righteousness is more than God's?" (35:2). Elihu's understanding adds nothing to what was said better by others before him. "Prosperity testifies to man's righteousness; calamity reveals his guilt." Job struggles for the conclusion that God reveals to the reader at the outset, that righteousness consists in how we face life, whether in prosperity or calamity.

Leslie Weatherhead enlarged the latter perspective in terms of Jesus' life and ministry. He begins by alleging that "Jesus took the dull metal of life's trivialities, life's accidents, and He changed them to shining gold by His attitude to them."[8] Elihu took the bold events in Job's experience as definitive for it all. Earlier the patriarch had prospered, so Elihu assumes that his life was then above reproach; now Job suffers, so he must be harboring grievous sin. Elihu overlooks, among other things, the importance of the commonplace, those hills and valleys that make up all but the little bit of life employed by mountain peaks and deep ravines.

Righteousness does not come and go, as Elihu suggests, in great leaps and relapses. At least that is not generally the case. More often, righteousness amounts to getting a little advantage here, a wedge there, some ground in another direction. It comes from living with God through life's routine, taking countless steps to achieve the desired result.

We would do much better with the big tests of life if we applied ourselves more to the smaller ones. A young man goes off to college, only to find that he has been thrown in with a thoroughly obnoxious roommate. Distracted from his studies, he considers dropping out of school. No one blames him in one sense because the roommate has made life virtually intolerable for him. The student, however, flounders primarily because of his lack of preparation rather than the difficult circumstance. He has not nurtured a lovingly firm attitude in the everyday routine and therefore finds it practically impossible to manage a genuinely severe test.

When we get away from Elihu's way of thinking, life takes on a much more realistic and practical dimension. We know that worthwhile things come to us through serious application. We look at the seasoned athlete and appreciate the months and years that have gone into his conditioning; we view the facilities of an expanding enterprise and realize the effort sustained by so many to make it possible; we listen to an orchestration and ponder the skills that have been so painstakingly blended to put it together. It makes sense that righteousness should come about in a similar manner.

Godliness is a lifelong process. The marks of the Master's hands are everywhere visible in the godly man: in his stalwart commitment to justice, his gentle compassion toward those in need, his perseverance with thankless tasks. Such signs of character take time and skill to bring about.

The godly man is also the growing person. Though we all leave much to be desired, God takes His time in correcting the condition. Godliness may be measured not so much as it approaches the ideal but, rather, as the progress we are making toward it. The righteous man travels the right road, regardless of how far he has come.

We have ample reason to be encouraged. Given time, God will accomplish with us what seems impossible at the moment. It is crucial to set the proper course, with God's help, and stick to it no matter how difficult it may seem at any particular point. One step at a time, one step after another—this characterizes the righteous man.

We again pick up Weatherhead's commentary: "Jesus always knew the right re-agent to use so that the nature of the happening could be changed to spiritual advantage.

He did not believe that everything that happened to Him was the will of God rigidly worked out."[9] In what sense were happenings not God's will "rigidly worked"? Jesus did not accept circumstances as He found them but creatively altered them in the service of God. Jesus discovered the sick and left them well, located the lonely and comforted them, unearthed sinners and saved them. Lives were changed after Jesus passed their way.

How did Jesus go about changing things? Weatherhead says that He introduced the "right re-agent . . . so that the nature of a happening could be changed to spiritual advantage." In other words, He contributed what was needed to transform a hindrance into a help.

Take two cases in point, the first a biblical one and the second an extra-biblical example. Jesus confronted a zealous persecutor of the church, fresh from a successful engagement in Jerusalem harassing believers and bound for a repeat performance at Damascus. Saul was not the kind of person who sits in the stands while others play the game of life. This had not been his character before the encounter with Jesus and it would not be thereafter. What Jesus did was to introduce a re-agent, which in this instance was a mission to the Gentile world. Saul left off persecuting the church to turn his boundless energies toward evangelizing the world.

Jesus uses various re-agents depending on the nature of the case. A friend of mine has attained an extraordinary academic discipline, but admits that he had had little patience with those in his field less rigorous. And this attitude limited his service. Eventually he underwent an extensive operation to rebuild a hip deformed at birth. Thereafter he had to follow a demanding schedule of rehabilitation that caused excruciating pain. This proved to be the re-agent that helped him to empathize with others and enriched his service on their behalf.

Elihu apparently was unwilling to take the time to work with life. He desires instant righteousness and frets when Job tries to find some re-agent that will help him live a godly life. The patriarch looks for a handle to his distressing situation so that even this might speak to the glory of God.

We do not know whether Job had a rejoinder in mind or simply meant to ignore this final attack from his associates. The division between them had grown with the discussion until Elihu was shouting at him across a yawning chasm. Such is the disparity between genuine faith and credulity and so little do they have in common.

The scene is set for God to intervene. Who will be exonerated? Will it be the patriarch or his associates? The Almighty will have the final word.

Questions for Study and Discussion

1. Elihu belatedly joins the discussion (chapters 32–37) because of his youth. Also, he is angered because the others offered no satisfactory answers to Job. Discuss what opportunities, or lack of them, that the youth of your church have for contributing their opinions. How can a church blend the enthusiasm of young people with the experience of the adults?

2. Distinguish between faith and credulity. How does Job illustrate the former and Elihu the latter? Discuss other instances of faith and credulity, either from biblical or extra-biblical accounts.

3. Some liken faith to sitting in a chair in anticipation that it will hold. I prefer to think of faith in God as resembling the trust we place in another person. What difference is there between these two analogies? Is this difference significant?

4. Faith should be thought of in reference to someone and for some purpose. (Thus, "by faith" Moses kept the Passover.)

With this in mind, what was the nature of Job's faith? And how did it differ from what Elihu demanded of him?

5. "Now faith is the assurance of things hoped for, the conviction of things not seen" (Heb. 11:1). What implications can you draw from this verse to the discussion of certainty? How does it bear on the topic of righteousness?

Self-Acceptance

Goal: To develop a healthy and constructive attitude toward oneself.

Then the Lord answered
Job out of the whirlwind and
said, "Who is this that darkens
counsel by words without knowledge?
Now gird up your loins like
a man, and I will ask you,
and you instruct Me!"
(Job 38:1–3).

The storm Elihu saw gathering, which he used to document his thinking, now broke with all its fury. The gusts whipped the pathetic figure of Job and the small circle of associates standing nearby. Suddenly it became an effort for them to speak against the wind to extend their already lengthy discussion.

God had a question for Job. Before, the patriarch had been demanding answers from God, but now the situation is reversed. "Who is this that darkens counsel by words without knowledge?" the Almighty inquires of the pathetic figure. "Now gird up your loins like a man, and I will ask you, and you instruct Me!"

"Who are you?" God was saying to the patriarch. Who am I? Job had to ask himself as he reached down into the private springs of his personality for an answer. Who am I to raise such profound issues from such a limited perspective? Who am I that shifts the burden of proof on the Almighty?

Job

The meaning of Job's name has been lost to antiquity. Some think it signifies an "object of enmity" and others conjecture that it indicates "he who turns." Perhaps, in an experiential sense, Job had to decide for himself, to reach back and take a long look and come up with the significance.

Self-acceptance can be a much more difficult task than we suppose. I recall a person who, following a laryngectomy, could not reconcile himself to life without a larynx. He would try to imagine that the surgery had never taken place, and whenever the truth of the matter forced itself on him he would retreat weeping into an adjoining room. He simply could not accept himself under the circumstances that had developed.

Of course, the problem of self-acceptance involves much more than our physical state of being. Years ago I met a zealous young man with an unenviable trait. At an early age he had received more recognition than many do in a lifetime, and he unrealistically assumed that recognition ought to be extended to him whether he deserved it or not. He kept thinking of himself as a prodigy when in fact he had become an obnoxious bore.

Job had a peculiarly difficult situation. Having become accustomed to thinking of himself in the midst of splendor, he had to settle for the refuse heap. Every sensitivity within Job cried out to reject his circumstances. Imagine his body running with sores, the rancid smell, the unrelenting itch, and his matted hair. Worse yet, his former serenity had been replaced by less comforting emotions. He wields his potsherd in disgust. Wretched flesh, despicable creature! If God would only lay it to rest!

A young lady, who had been horribly disfigured at birth, suggests the road to self-acceptance, which Job had to travel. From the middle of her face gaped a large cavity. Her eyes turned to the sides as if to object to the horror between them. Otherwise, she was alert and strong. Can we appreciate how difficult her task of self-acceptance? Yet she achieved where others fail. Out of an early and continuing experience with God, she learned that because God accepted her she could accept herself.

The first step Job took toward self-acceptance was to appreciate God's thorough knowledge of all things, including the subtle character of his own identity. "Tell Me, if you have understanding, who set its [the earth's] measurements . . . or who stretched the line on it . . . or who laid its cornerstone" (38:4–6). Certainly not Job, but the Almighty grasps such things.

God knows us from the inside out. Every aspect of our personalities is open to His gaze. Our masks please and amuse our friends, but we cannot fool God. We hide our guilt from others lest they use it against us, but all our secrets are known to the Almighty. We have no fine clothes to impress Him, no clever remarks to win Him over, and no gifts to court His favor. We cannot hide from God's searching gaze.

If we cannot conceal ourselves from God, all masquerade is pointless. We might as well take a long look at what God sees. At that point self-acceptance originates.

God's discourse continues. "Have you entered into the springs of the sea?" He inquires of Job, "or have you walked in the recesses of the deep?" (38:16). The patriarch's breadth suffered from comparison with God's. Where can God be found? Everywhere. The idea of divine omnipresence staggers us. He is everywhere! He rides the sun as it breaks through the distant horizon; He peers from behind the shade cast from a stalwart tree; He parts the grass at our feet. God moves through His creation like an invisible breeze sending ripples over a placid lake.

Self-acceptance occurs in some particular context rather than as an abstraction. Here an appreciation of the omnipresence of God can be of immeasurable help. It is because we expect Him to be there that we can accept our own involvement instead of fleeing into fantasy.

God takes the patriarch one step further. "Can you bind the chains of Pleiades, or loose the cords of Orion?" (38:31). Is there anyone who can match the power of God? Our sense of inadequacy on the one hand and responsibility on the other hinders us from self-acceptance. We sing a hymn about being "such a worm" rather than face the fact that we are humans. But God counters, "Now gird up your loins like a man." Get on with self-acceptance. Get on with it because the Almighty takes such dust to fashion destiny out of it. Believe God for the impossible.

The Almighty introduces Job to Himself. Through God's omniscience, the patriarch realizes that he cannot hide; through His omnipresence, he must not shirk; through His omnipotence, he can achieve. God encourages Job to look within, without, and ahead, and where these lines of consideration converge, he finds himself. Self-acceptance turns out to be a matter of introspection, inspection, and projection. I am what I sense myself to be, qualified by how I act and what I anticipate.

We gain a remarkably dynamic picture of ourselves as a result of the investigation up to this point. We are a peculiar combination of the past, present, and future—those forces that have conditioned us, the context in which we live, and the goals we assume.

Coincidence of Wills

We could terminate the discussion of self-acceptance at this point except for some related concerns that touch on a healthy attitude toward self. C. S. Lewis observed, "If the thing we like doing is, in fact, the thing God wants us to do, yet that is not our reason for doing it; it remains a mere happy coincidence."[1] We can derive four combinations based on desire and performance from Lewis's comment:

Want and do God's will
Want but do not God's will
Do not want but do God's will
Do not want and do not God's will

By following through these options, we can discover something of how our lives intertwine with the will of God.

We acknowledge first those who want and do God's will. Lewis describes this as a "happy coincidence." I enjoy playing tennis but never so much as when I have someone who equally appreciates the sport. Such compatibility amounts to a happy coincidence. No one would think to inquire whether one had to give up his pleasure to satisfy the other. If anything, the original interest increases from the interplay with someone similarly motivated.

Perhaps this accounts for Paul's renewed efforts in preaching the gospel at Corinth. We are told that when Silas and Timothy arrived, the apostle began "devoting himself completely to the word, solemnly testifying to the Jews that Jesus was the Christ" (Acts 18:5). As Lewis would have it, there was a happy coincidence of purpose that resulted in an intensified ministry.

We sense that there are others who want to do God's will but fail miserably in their efforts. Paul described such an experience in his own life, "For the good that I wish, I do not do; but I practice the very evil that I do not wish" (Rom. 7:19). "Wretched man that I am," he adds. There was no *happy* coincidence here but wretchedness instead. There was a coincidence of wills but a divergence in practice.

Others do not care to do God's will but end up doing so. Balaam provides us with such a case in point. Balak had called upon him to curse the people of Israel and promised a rich reward for his services. The angel who meets Balaam assumes the role of an adversary and subsequently when Balaam hopes to earn his stipend, his words fall out as a blessing instead of a curse (Num. 22–24). Thus was God's will served although begrudgingly.

We often find persons doing good acts from the wrong motives. Perhaps some needy person benefits from the efforts of another seeking only to gain the recognition of his peers. The latter gives providing that a conspicuous memorial will recall his generosity. He does God's will, but that is not his intent.

We come finally to those who persist in opposing the Almighty. There comes to mind a young boy who was brutally beaten. Several older boys had pinned his arms behind him while administering blow after blow to his unprotected midriff. His counselor subsequently discovered the lad doubled up with pain, terrified to divulge who his attackers had been and at his wit's end.

God actually brought good out of this situation through a deep relationship that developed between the youngster and his counselor but not because of any concern shown by the older boys. Rather, they seemed to be pleased with what they had done.

The preferred option is when we experience a happy coincidence of wills—God's will and our own—and when we are able to successfully implement life to please God and ourselves. Then we discover what it means to be resting in the will of God, rejoicing in His goodness, and serving His purpose.

Taking Risks

So long as Job could lay the burden of proof on the Almighty, he had to risk little of himself. But when God demanded that he gird up his loins like a man, the patriarch had to get involved and accept the risks that were implied.

A fragile youth enrolled in a wilderness hardship course. Soon after he arrived at camp the director had him slopping through mud up to his waist. "Why did I ever let myself in for this?" the boy thought to himself. During the days that followed, he would have quit dozens of times if he could have slipped off undetected. However, he managed a thoroughly unnerving obstacle course, survived a three-day solo hike, ran until his legs threatened to drop off, and, in the process, developed a more positive attitude toward himself.

Anton Boisen tells of a young man from a southern state who was raised in a Baptist minister's home. At an early age he enlisted in the army and uncritically took on the code of his associates. It was not until some nine years after retirement from the military that the deep-seated conflict between his early instruction and later accommodation began to assert itself. Illusion virtually eclipsed reality for him, as he imagined himself an emissary to reconcile God and Satan and to bring in the millennium.[2] His trouble began when he started to insulate his early faith from the ongoing realities of the military experience. The man who risks nothing is in danger of losing everything.

God's summons to Job resembles a military inspection more than a casual conversation. He wants to see how Job measures up after his experience. Imagine the patriarch braced at attention while God's expert eyes survey him from head to foot. Listen to his pointed responses as the Almighty judges their accuracy. Better for Job to have struggled with his dilemma earlier than to be faced with his neglect at this late time.

Jesus told a parable (Matt. 25:14–30) about a man ready to undertake a long journey who entrusted his property to servants. Upon his return, he asked them for an accounting. Each of the stewards showed a reasonable profit, except for one who, fearing the austerity of his master, kept his portion secure. He now returned the full sum (no more and no less) and received the reprimand, "You wicked, lazy slave, you knew that I reap where I did not sow, and gather where I scattered no seed. Then you ought to have put my money in the bank, and on my arrival I should have received my money back with interest" (vv. 26–27). A man may try and fail, but the overly cautious man loses by default.

Persistence

We ought to anticipate opposition, discouragement, and apathy. The world seldom urges us on with enthusiastic applause. We must persevere as a trained athlete under the watchful eye of his coach.

A. Graham Ikin suggests that essentially there are only three responses to opposition: break out (anti-social), break down (neuroticism), or break through (constructive progress). He adds, "The difference between break out, break down and break through may hinge on that ability to hold out just a few seconds longer to draw on invisible, but very real reinforcements, which come when the need is real and our commitment to the 'job in hand' is sincere enough."[3] We need to resist the erosion of our purpose for a moment longer, to draw upon God's grace, and experience His deliverance. That additional moment we persevere may make all the difference between success and failure.

The unfortunate alternatives to perseverance are to cop out or buckle under. Flight takes many disguises. One of the more common and difficult to correct is religious rationalization. We become so busy serving God in general that we are of no use to any person in particular. We crowd our evenings with meetings, programmed to ease our guilt for being unavailable to others or to the leading of God's Spirit, and we perpetuate the most irrelevant tasks while the world weeps over its open wounds.

Even the body may cooperate with our self-deception, translating our fears into physical symptoms, as with a certain woman who would become violently ill in the presence of her husband. Instead of dealing with her marriage problems, she used her distress as an excuse for divorce. She fled her situation, preferring her neuroticism to responsible behavior.

On other occasions, we may shift the blame for our failure from ourselves to others or circumstances. We maintain that persons proved unresponsive or events were stacked against us, with the unfortunate result that we feel dismissed from any further obligation.

Ikin counsels us to face life as we find it and set a good course. Adverse winds will develop, and we can either lower the sail and drift, or we can tack into the wind. But only with the second option will we make headway.

Many times Job must have wanted to give up, but still he plodded ahead. He picked up an insight here, a confidence there, and pressed on. Distracted by his friends, he strained to steady his direction. Overwhelmed by God's presence, he stumbled forward like a man coming out of a deep sleep.

God's interrogation made Job painfully aware of his struggle. "Behold, I am insignificant," he protested, "what can I reply to Thee?" (40:4). What indeed! You are a man, created in the image of God, the object of the Almighty's concern. Do not grovel like a senseless beast, but see the majesty of God and recall that you were meant to commune with Him. Look up and take heart. Look within and take inventory. Do not despise what the Almighty has done and expects to do with your life and for His glory.

Questions for Study and Discussion

1. Jesus taught "You shall love your neighbor as yourself" (Matt. 19:19). If we hate ourselves, can we actually love another? How does Jesus' injunction bear upon self-acceptance?

2. In another context, I stated that "man's self-image is the measure of his potential. . . . He is capable of a predatory life, imitating the jungle law of survival" (*Psychology in the Psalms*, p. 25). Does this quotation tie into the general theme of the book and the specific topic of self-acceptance? Why or why not?

3. An opposite danger is that man sometimes thinks of himself as God. Why does this happen? What are the dangers of man assuming to speak for God on matters not revealed in Scripture? Can you cite any examples?

4. It is said that we must keep a delicate balance between God's transcendence and immanence. Does the account of Job illustrate the wisdom of this opinion? Are there other examples that come to mind in this connection?

5. What is the meaning and significance of a "coincidence of wills"? Does this idea resolve some problems that people struggle with? If so, what are they?

6. An old adage states, "nothing ventured, nothing gained." How might this fit into the discussion of taking risks? Are there also unnecessary risks that persons take on out of a false sense of commitment? How may one distinguish between legitimate and illegitimate risks?

Devotion to God

Goal: To discover how to intercede before God on behalf of others.

Now therefore, take
for yourselves seven bulls
and seven rams, and go to My servant
Job, and offer up a burnt offering
for yourselves, and My servant Job
will pray for you. For I will
accept him so that I may not do
with you according to your
folly, because you have not
spoken of Me what is right, as
My servant Job has
(Job 42:8).

Job stood out as the paragon of virtue. God said as much to Satan. Yet, when calamity struck, he tried to acquit himself at the Almighty's expense. "Will you condemn

Me that you may be justified?" God incredulously asks
him. The patriarch was right in rejecting the hellish por-
trait Elihu tried to paint of him, but wrong in pushing his
rectitude to the point of impugning the loving Father.

God's reprimand of Job brings us to consider more
carefully the implications of living with His presence in
view. This theme has been woven throughout our discussion but comes to a climax where God breaks His silence
to speak with Job and his associates.

Sensing God's Presence

Edgar Dickie suggests that we have two contrasting
methods for exploring the world in which we live;
through our senses and by way of empathy. He says of the
latter, "By sympathy—or by empathy—we 'go through it
all' with another person."[1] We put ourselves in the other
person's place and act with his welfare in mind.

Jesus taught that "whatever you want others to do for
you, do so for them" (Matt. 7:12). This seems to be the
crux of the matter: to act with concern for others.

We may prove forgetful of God also. We lose the sense
of His presence, speak as though He were not listening
in, and act as if He were not concerned.

Suffering tends to monopolize our thinking. It calls
upon all our reserves and crowds out the attention we
might otherwise extend to others. Job was struggling to
manage his own situation; God was being pushed into the
background.

The patriarch's associates compounded the problem
for him. They kept hammering away at the plight of the
pathetic man and the guilt they supposed had solicited it.
They portrayed God as remote and resolute in His determination to punish poor Job. There was little in their

words or behavior to suggest that the Almighty might be standing alongside to assist the suffering man.

Job seemed caught up in the polemic. He argued as though his life depended on the outcome. And when he finally tired of the interchange, it was not to recover his sensitivity to God's presence. It was not until the Almighty spoke that Job was alerted either to his problem or God's solution. It was as if God shouted to get the patriarch's attention after His whispers had so long fallen on deaf ears.

Some have argued that we "practice the presence of God" as a preventative to a plight such as Job's. It amounts to consciously living with God's concerns in view until such time that it becomes our natural approach to life. It resembles the reflex action familiar to the athlete who drills himself to the point that during the intense competition of the game he automatically does what is called for. He no longer has to stop and think what should be done.

Practicing the presence of God also implies an attitude of trust and rejoicing. There comes a sense of peace and desire for celebration that surrounds even the most irritating situation. It is less an escape from the trying circumstance than facing it with our hand in the hand of the living God.

In practicing the presence of God we seek to bring every straying thought into submission to the Almighty. We long to think God's thoughts after Him, to see God's world in its totality and every detail in its proper relationship to the rest. We heed Paul's admonition: "Finally, brethren, whatever is true, whatever is honorable, whatever is right, whatever is pure, whatever is lovely, whatever is of good repute, if there is any excellence and if anything worthy of praise, let your mind dwell on these things" (Phil. 4:8).

"Practice makes perfect." The example of Job reminds us that we must keep on cultivating the presence of God or experience a lapse as a result. There is no place for complacency in a successful spiritual pilgrimage. Today's victories are the prelude to tomorrow's endeavor.

Realizing God's Purpose

Job wondered what God was up to. The divine purpose seemed obscure if not utterly incomprehensible. Job desperately wanted to get a sure handle on life.

Leslie Weatherhead provides us with a guideline for knowing God's intent: "God's will is to replace ignorance with knowledge, folly with wisdom, and sin with holiness."[2] God takes no satisfaction in our ignorance. He wants to substitute knowledge for ignorance, and Job seems to have sensed this. His associates discouraged him in the quest for understanding by simplistic analyses or solutions, but the patriarch persevered in good faith.

Paul warned his readers, "See to it that no one takes you captive through philosophy and empty deception" (Col. 2:8). Some have taken this to mean that we should shun knowledge as such. But such is not the case; it is rather reprobate, twisted knowledge we ought to avoid. The genuine quest for truth brings on God's blessing. We may count on it as commensurate with the Almighty's purpose, regardless of any qualifying considerations. We need not be in doubt at this point.

God likewise desires wisdom in preference to folly. Wisdom conveys the ideal of skill. It refers not so much to what we know as to how well we apply that knowledge to various situations.

One man who lacked wisdom was a pleasant fellow in many respects but quite irresponsible. He would work only enough to meet his current needs and was always unprepared for emergencies. His poor sense of priorities further compounded the problem. He would spend money needed for his family on alcoholic beverages and other indulgences. Eventually he lost his family, home, and respectability.

The wise man behaves differently. He meets his pressing obligations, prepares for any eventuality, and respects the needs of others. He also enjoys the blessing of God for his effort. The Almighty always opts for wisdom instead of folly.

Job was the paradigm of wisdom, regardless of his shortcomings. God declared this to be the case. Job attempted to apply such knowledge as he had to the case at hand, while his associates charged around like bulls in the proverbial china shop. Job took the divinely appointed course, away from folly, to gain wisdom.

God also prefers holiness to sin. Sin is any failure to conform to God's perfect will. It is essentially religious in character, an offense against the Almighty, no matter what else may be implied.

The Almighty instructed Moses to say to the congregation, "You shall be holy, for I the Lord your God am holy" (Lev. 19:2). Peter similarly observed that "you are a chosen race, a royal priesthood, a holy nation, a people for God's own possession, that you may proclaim the excellencies of Him who has called you out of darkness into His marvelous light" (I Peter 2:9).

The people of Israel held back at the foot of Mount Sinai in recognition of the holy character of the Almighty and their own sinfulness, while Moses climbed the mountain to intercede on their behalf. It reminds us of a

chasm between God and man that is being bridged only
by the grace of God. Holiness is standing with God, at His
invitation, and by His help.

The result may be seen as piety. The genuine godly
man is at the same time the essentially good man. He is no
longer squandering a godly heritage, in the process of
losing whatever good inclinations others may have fostered in his life. He is becoming conformed to the will of
God, whether at a painfully slow pace or with great leaps
and bounds.

The Almighty agitates for knowledge in preference to
ignorance, wisdom to folly, and holiness to sin, and He
does so out of love for us. God acts in love. He consider-
ately lays the foundation of the earth, measures the extent
of the universe, encloses the seas, wraps the world with
clouds, girdles it with darkness, rotates the earth in place,
and rules with equity (38:4–5, 8–9, 12). We do not know
the details of how God is working at any given moment,
any more than Job could grasp the nature of the disaster
befalling him. But we can be certain that God does what
He does out of genuine compassion.

"The goodness of God . . . does not consist in [His]
desire to cushion His children from the hardships and
pains of life, but in a providential interest in us, which we
can trace in the Bible and experience in our personal
lives, aimed at our moral development."[3] In God's purpose the good of people is more important than the pleasures they experience. His word reveals this to be so and
our experience confirms it.

An especially pampered child well illustrates this concept. While enjoying much of the good things of life, the
child lacks even the basic sensitivities one expects to find
in another. The child's crass behavior seems purposefully
offensive. The parents have given this child the impres-

sion that the world exists for personal convenience. Such a persuasion is ultimately broken against the hard realities of life. But God is not so cruel as to shore up such fantasies in the minds of His children. Instead, He helps them face life for what it holds and find fulfillment in the process.

What is God's purpose for us? It is to understand life, develop skills in living, and foster concern for the welfare of others. Why does He desire these qualities? Because of His matchless love. He embraces our lives in His loving concern.

Tapping God's Power

How can we realize God's power in our lives? Job was concerned with how to cope with his trial as well as understanding what God meant to accomplish through it. The two concerns were inseparable in his thinking, as they should be in ours.

Wayne Oates exposes the issue for us by describing a fearful woman who could not bear to think that God might punish her. She asked her minister to intercede on her behalf in regard to her persistent back pains and her dread that her marriage was failing. The pastor responded frankly by telling her "that the miracle would come in her facing and accepting the necessity of struggle, and sincerely searching for God in the quietness of her own privacy when she was away from all other persons, including the minister himself."[4] The woman hoped to tap God's power without getting personally involved with Him or in resolving the problems she faced. But the pastor wisely counseled her to seek God and face the prospect of struggling through her difficulties by His grace.

The woman naturally turned to the concerned minister. His warm smile and firm grip seemed more assuring at the moment than the less tangible assurance of God's presence. We ought not to feel guilty for wanting the encouragement of some other person, but we must not allow that person to get in our way of approach to the Almighty. It is God's power we want to experience, and, to receive it, we must tap into the original source.

The woman hoped for a miracle but she little understood the context for miracles. She had fallen back on childish responses to her problems. Richard Sternbach explains what happens in such instances: "As we fall back on our childhood responses and attitudes, we call for help, for the good parent to take away the hurt. We are sorry, we promise to be good, and the punishment should stop. But the hurt stays with us. It seems as though we are unloved and abandoned—the good parent does not help us."[5] Thus an infantile response springs up to choke off mature growth and the effective working of God in our lives. The woman's pastor appreciated the problem and urged his parishioner to opt instead for spiritual growth. God does not perform miracles to satisfy childish behavior but to attest to our developing maturity.

A childish reliance on a parental figure diminishes personal responsibility and proves self-defeating. Such a retreat into the artlessness of infancy rejects the obligations that come with an appreciation of the complexities of our world. It fails to tap the power of God because it ignores the world as the place where God demonstrates that power.

This is not to minimize God's power in the least. It is rather to sense afresh the greater extent of His power as it relates to a world that has grown in our understanding. We do not expect less but more from God as a result. But we see more clearly the source of that power and our own responsibility as channels of it.

We tap the power of God by reaching out to Him. There is no other. Job's associates were at best no substitute for the Almighty. They attempted from time to time to play the surrogate, but their performance lacked credibility. Job knew that his case was before the Almighty, and the arguments of his associates did not sway him.

We tap the power of God when *we* reach out to Him. We cannot expect others to do this for us. We have to resist those who would usurp our role in that regard. Job is our example. He was determined to make his own peace with God and not accept something manufactured by his associates.

The prophet Isaiah reminds us,

> Behold, the Lord's hand is not so short
> That it cannot save;
> Neither is His ear so dull
> That it cannot hear (Isa. 59:1).

We may anticipate God's power to sustain us in the severest of trials, but we do so as persons struggling with our problems and resting in His grace. It offers no solace to those attempting to retreat to childish ways.

Realizing God's Pain

Kazah Kitamori reports that "the heart of the gospel was revealed to me as the pain of God."[6] We shall approach the subject of God's suffering reverently, first by way of contrast and then to view it in its stark splendor. "Before we leave this subject of the strange providence which allows God's world, and even the short span of a single human life, to be an arena in which divine and malignant forces wage grim battle, we must remember that, great as the sufferer's pains so often are, God Himself is the great sufferer."[7] We know something of pain but God has delved into its depths.

God in Christ experienced the suffering of crucifixion and other trials of human existence. What made His agony greater in these experiences was His unusual perception of events. He caught glimpses of the future, dimensions of the present, and aspects of the past that escape the rest of us.

There was also something unique to God's suffering. The prophet Isaiah put it this way:

> But He was pierced through for our transgressions,
> He was crushed for our iniquities;
> The chastening for our well-being fell upon Him,
> And by His scourging we are healed (Isa. 53:5).

The measure of God's pain is the distance from our sin to His salvation.

Because so much is beyond our grasp it seems almost foolish to focus on this unique dimension to divine suffering. But it is important that we do so. While we cannot thoroughly comprehend its nature, we nonetheless explore it as a clue to our own experience.

We first begin to appreciate the uniqueness of God's suffering with the fact that sin inevitably reaps suffering. You frequently hear someone say, "I am not hurting anyone but myself." Actually, that is never true because sin hurts others as well. Hurt to others invariably follows on the heels of sin.

Pain is deeply ingrained in life about us and in ways we seldom think about. The deplorable condition of overcrowded prisons is one example. Few stop to question whether so many should be incarcerated in one facility, which intensifies frustration and violence among prison-

ers. We react to news of a prison revolt but soon slip back
into a complacent indifference.

Sin has succeeded in inflicting the world with immeasurable pain. Astonishingly God took all that sin on
Himself and experienced it in His own flesh. He was
bruised for our iniquities. The agony that causes us to
turn our eyes elsewhere, He took in full stride.

God suffered so that human sin and suffering could be
transformed into salvation and health. This transformation is available to all who will receive it. A gift is never
ours until we accept it.

Imagine a person holding on to a rope from which
another dangles precariously. The rope begins to cut into
his hands and blood drips from his fingers. Still he pulls
the rope until his friend has reached safety beside him.
Not once did he relax his grip as long as the other remained in danger. So it is with God; He hangs on until the
work has been completed and the last believing soul is
safe forevermore.

One thing more needs to be said in rounding out the
picture of God's suffering. George Buttrick reminds us
that pain "is parasitic . . . because we could not know
pain except for prior joy, but also because in the Cross it
has been changed so that now it is God's agent in redemp-
tion. It is doomed because of that transformation."[7] John
promised in the same vein, "He shall wipe away every
tear from their eyes; and there shall no longer be any
death; there shall no longer be any mourning, or crying,
or pain; the first things have passed away" (Rev. 21:4).
When sin finally is removed from life's stage, so will its
companion, suffering, be removed.

In response, how can we better devote ourselves to
God and respect His will for our lives? Is God present?

Then do not ignore Him. Has He a purpose for your life?
Then seek it out. Does He provide strength for you to live
by? Then make use of it. Does He accept suffering on our
behalf? Then gladly accept His sacrifice and do not flinch
from pain in your own life.

Questions for Study and Discussion

1. It has been said, "Love God and do as you please."
Another observed that if we genuinely love the Almighty we
will do as He pleases. How do these associated ideas help
summarize the account of Job to this point?

2. What does it mean "to practice the presence of God"?
How would you explain this concept to a child?

3. There are times when our need is not so much to know
God's will as to do it. How does this statement get at the
discussion of God's purpose for man? How would you correct
or qualify those things attributed to God's will? Give examples.

4. How would you guide a person who wants to experience
the power of God in his life? Are there misconceptions of His
power which you would want to clear up in the process? Can
you illustrate the power of God from your own experience or
that of others?

5. Kazah Kitamori identifies the pain of God as the key to
life. After studying this chapter, have you changed your opinion regarding God's suffering? Is the issue in clearer focus, or is
it clouded by additional considerations?

Ministry of
Reconciliation

Goal: To foster
dedication to the Almighty and
to His purposes.

Will you really annul
My judgment? Will you condemn Me
that you may be justified?
(Job 40:8).

God turned His attention momentarily to Job's associates. "You have not spoken of Me what is right," the Almighty charged them. Nor had they ministered to the patriarch as they ought to have done. They had misrepresented God and failed their friend.

Job might have been tempted to taunt his associates at this point, to return some of the hatefulness they had shown him. But God had something else in mind. He anticipated that Job would intercede for the rest.

On Behalf of Others

Hans Küng observes, "The priesthood of the believer is not just a private relationship between him and his God. . . . [It] must ultimately be to the advantage of all men, must always be a service of one's fellow men and of the world."[1] We do not seek reconciliation for ourselves alone but for others as well.

In response to God's invitation, Job ministered to his associates. The man berated, ridiculed, and defamed by his friends now intercedes on their behalf. Job reflected the spirit of Jesus who prayed, when agonizing from the cross, "Father forgive them; for they do not know what they are doing" (Luke 23:34).

Three factors qualified Job for his ministry of reconciliation: his recognition of others, his understanding of their need, and his stance before God. The patriarch took his associates seriously. He kept them in full view and weighed their words for whatever truth they might have held. He refused to turn them off and retreat to his private world.

As we include others in our lives the possibility of service remains. It is that prospect, even after all efforts seem to fail, that enables a person to tolerate the abuse he may be receiving. He imagines that God is able to break in at any moment to redeem the situation. He does not intend to quit while God still may be working.

Job suffered long with his associates, but often that is what it takes to really get to know someone. At times we must deal with individuals who are opinionated and difficult to associate with. The thought of seeing them again after a time makes us feel tense and defensive. But we cannot afford to reject them for that reason, seeing that God may have some service for us to render to them. And for all we know, they may have a valid complaint about us and a concern for the Almighty to minister to us through them.

We must develop awareness to the needs of others so that we can pray intelligently for them. Job's friends could have been less concerned for his repentance and more responsive to his need. They found a man gasping for spiritual life but, instead, criticized him for his shortness of breath.

Persons experience a variety of needs, some of which seem more pressing than others. Our own sense of their priority of needs may differ, and they may resent our efforts to bypass some felt need to get at what we understand to be the more critical concern. The general rule, however, is to begin with their felt need, even if it means to set it carefully aside before focusing on what we think to be the more critical problem. This allows us to build a trust relationship and to enlarge the opportunity for service in the process.

Persons cannot be served in a vacuum. When we minister to them in a set of circumstances, as they perceive those circumstances, they will more readily accept our assistance. When we fail to grapple with their needs, real or imaginary, we fail to serve them. And a ministry rendered is only one that is a ministry received.

The succinct comment of Scripture is that "the Lord accepted Job" (42:9). He enjoyed a position from which he could effectively intercede on behalf of his associates. He was on what some older devotional literature describes as "praying ground." He had a spiritual advantage his associates lacked.

One young man asked his girlfriend to help him out of his spiritual dilemma. Sensing her own inadequacy, she replied, "If I can find my way, I will be able to help you as well." Neither of these young people seem to have made substantial spiritual progress to this day. Neither of them had or have gained any spiritual leverage by which to help the other.

Everyone has need, but some find their way to God more easily than others. They have discovered how the Almighty meets their needs and can guide others in need. Job was such a person. He recognized those about him, their plight, and his access to the Almighty—not for himself alone but for others.

Seizing the Opportunity

The ministry of reconciliation begins with a positive attitude concerning the situation in which we find ourselves. Though we cannot ignore the disagreeable aspects, we believe that God can turn even these to serve His gracious purposes. We accept what befalls us as being allowed by God and within the domain of His complex good. As Paul could say, "I am overflowing with joy in all our affliction," and "Now I rejoice in my sufferings for your sake" (II Cor. 7:4; Col. 1:24).

The apostle saw divine opportunity in all of life. Even the most adverse circumstances seemed to hold some anticipated benefit. Driven from one city, he went on courageously to another. Apprehended, he secured permission to speak to the multitude trying to do him injury. On a ship driven by a violent storm, he comforted those with him. Imprisoned, he preached to his jailors. Each new day held another opportunity. Paul's optimism reflected the psalmist's proclamation, "This is the day

which the Lord has made; let us rejoice and be glad in it"
(Ps. 118:24).

Job's case similarly illustrates the importance of a
favorable attitude toward life. Albion King reduces the
patriarch's success to five propositions: "belief in a judgment beyond death, the intrinsic value of moral integrity,
the disciplinary value of suffering and its stimulus to
human progress, and suffering as a pathway to God."[2]
These points can be profitably drawn together here by
way of summary. The Scripture solemnly announces,
"And inasmuch as it is appointed for men to die once, and
after this comes judgment" (Heb. 9:27). A popular adage
assures us of two things, death and taxes, but the biblical
expression is death and judgment. After death is judgment when every man shall give account of what he has
done with the opportunities extended to him.

Job lived with the prospect of judgment in view. And
by word and deed he encouraged his associates to do
likewise. This was the first key to his successful ministry.

He also appreciated the intrinsic value of moral integrity. The person lives best who lives according to what he
ought to do. Even if there were no future judgment, the
man of principle has taken the preferred way. He en-
riches the lives of others and himself. Job was persuaded
of this, and it, too, contributed to his ministry of reconciliation.

King's remaining points have to do with the role of
suffering, suggesting what a large contribution it made in
the patriarch's life. He points out first of all how pain can
help disciple us. Suppose we were to recollect all of those
events that substantially influenced our lives over the
past year. In all probability, they would include the full
sweep of happenings, both unfavorable to favorable. God
disciples us through life's contrasts, not by means of unin-

terrupted good fortune. Pain as well as pleasure provides occasions for man to learn life's values, and the two together give us unmatched instruction.

Pain, by its demand for attention, also turns the wheels of progress. Much of our technological gain stems from the war years, where the urgency of human combat spurred us to action. We tend to give our pleasures a higher priority than human needs until some painful experience causes us to reconsider. That "does not mean, to reiterate, that God hands out a cancer because a man has been lustful. It means that man is put into a universe in which he slowly and surely discovers that life will only work out successfully in one way, and that is God's way."[3] When man is slow to learn, it is not for the lack of lesson material. Pain dogs our steps as a reminder of the progress the Almighty would have us make.

Finally, pain leads us to God. Through suffering we may turn from indifference to a deliberate quest for the Almighty. And we may find that this was what we had been looking for all along. This was what Job discovered in the end.

We have no way to get ahead but to go on. We must take life and turn it to our advantage. The equation is terribly simple but unnervingly right. It is essential for seizing life's opportunities. We go with God into a promising future.

Benefiting from Service

What of Job? How was God working with him as he ministered to others? "Not until Job sincerely prays for the welfare of those who had wrongly slandered and persecuted him is his repentance complete."[4] God had vindicated the patriarch, but not until he interceded for his associates was the victory truly his.

Job tasted the sweet nectar of triumph but not at the expense of others. Those who contended against him were the first to share in his good fortune. They sensed the rapture of Job's victory. From a sidewalk in Rome one can peer down through the Arch of Septimius Severus, across the Roman Forum, to the Arch of Titus. Here the Roman armies paraded to the accolade of the multitudes. Their conquests ignited a vicarious response. Thus may we think of the success of one man as that of all.

Job also experienced the satisfaction of empathy—to stand with men in their sin and failure. Likewise, on one occasion, Moses petitioned God to forgive the people or cross his own name as well from God's book of remembrance (Exod. 32:32). Though he did not share their guilt, he identified with them in their plight. He stood in the breach, much as Job was asked to do, to be a priest among men.

One grows under such circumstances, although feeling a strange ambivalence through it all. One might prefer an easier lot in life yet sense that this is more needful. Perhaps the discomfort experienced derives as much from personal growth as anything else. After stretching to meet the heavy demands of ministering to others, one discovers that he has been the one best served.

Not the least of Job's benefits was his experience of God's grace. After laboring His case against Job until he withered under the charges, God then swept the slate clean. It was the same Job, condemned in one sentence and extended leniency in the next.

What is it like to experience the grace of God? It is like medication quieting a distressed stomach, a lotion soothing a burned back, a word of comfort to a troubled mind, and so much more. The experience of grace comes upon us like the calm after a severe storm. Though we see in every direction the havoc and waste from our own misguided efforts, like up-rooted trees and debris, we can sense the fresh righteousness that God alone imputes to us. Like Job we can drink deeply from the cup of God's grace.

In addition, Job stood to profit from relationships now established on a more solid foundation. He could minister to others, and perhaps in the future they would minister to him. A bridge of empathy and understanding was constructed, over which either Job or his friends might travel to each other's assistance.

Life reminds us of a high, sheer wall that one person cannot scale alone. Only a human pyramid can get the first ones over, and later a rope is lowered to pick up the remaining climbers. "One thing is certain according to the Christian faith. You do not have to be able to manufacture courage all by yourself. There are two other resources—your neighbors and God."[5] We are able to overcome the greatest obstacle because of the cooperation of a reciprocal ministry.

The text of Job ends on an exceedingly pragmatic note, as William Ward explains: "The most important answer it gives is a practical one—how to go out and live a satisfying life in the face of hardship and disaster. Religion is not so much a philosophy as a way of life."[6] The emphasis is on *doing*. It is not that what we think is unimportant, since thoughts are the source of appropriate activity. If we serve the pantheon of the pagans, we employ their cunning and questionable devices to manipulate others. But if we strive to serve the living God, we then shall keep the concerns of others in our view.

Nonetheless, the accent falls on practice. Some coddle themselves as if the slightest stress would shatter them into a million pieces. Job learned otherwise. He came to see life as progress made possible by vigorous discipline and mutual assistance. He learned to trust God and himself in the most severe testing, knowing that God could work eternal good out of his perplexities.

The patriarch found pain a means for personal growth and witness. Life became more vital for him because of his experience with God in the midst of suffering. He discovered that pain could reveal God's purpose and release His power in the lives of those who were willing to seek His face.

Job concluded that life was indeed complex but also superlatively good. The easy formulas failed him, but the faithfulness of God came through as the sun's rays piercing the rain clouds. Mysteries of life would remain to puzzle him, but he could confidently trust that God would honor his determination to do right. Job's curiosity about life's ultimate questions would have to wait, while his stewardship of life's opportunities took precedence.

Whether banqueting joyously with his family or suffering on an ash heap, life for Job was cut out of one pattern in God's providence. We, too, can be certain of that fact in our lives and act upon it. With this conviction the saga of Job concludes and our own pilgrimage continues. We may make of life a jungle or a cathedral. The choice is ours.

Questions for Study and Discussion

1. It is commonly thought that the priesthood of believers means that each person may approach the Almighty without a go-between. In what sense is this popular understanding correct? In what way is it inadequate?

2. What were the qualifications of Job's ministry of reconciliation? Is one of these more critical than the others, or are they all equally essential?

3. All solutions have beginnings. How does this thought tie into the discussion of seizing our opportunities for intercession? Does it open any other avenues of thought for you to explore?

4. In serving, we are best served. What truth is there to this old adage? How is it illustrated in the experience of Job?

5. What practical significance have you gained from reading the Book of Job? Do you anticipate that your perspective on life and behavior will be altered? Are there ideas you would especially like to share with others? If so, what are they, with whom would you care to share them, and for what reasons?

6. "Life is cut out of one pattern in God's providence." Does this quotation sum up the thesis of the Book of Job? Is there an alternative theme which you prefer? Write a brief summary that you could share with someone interested in what the Book of Job is all about.

Notes

1. As the World Turns

1. J. Richard Spann, ed., *The Church and Social Responsibility*, p. 45.
2. C. S. Lewis, *The Problem of Pain*, pp. 110–11.
3. J. B. Phillips, *Your God Is Too Small*, p. 9.
4. George Bernanos, *The Diary of a Country Priest*, p. 163.
5. J. B. Phillips, *Plain Christianity*, p. 49.
6. Morris Inch, *Psychology in the Psalms*, p. 99.
7. C. S. Lewis, *The Problem of Pain*, p. 111.

2. Lead on Living

1. Dietrich Bonhoeffer, *Creation and Fall and Temptation*, p. 40.
2. Ibid., p. 39.
3. Sten Stenson, *Sense and Nonsense in Religion*, p. 23.
4. Edward Madden and Peter Hare, *Evil and the Concept of God*, p. 70.
5. Wayne Oates, *The Revelation of God in Human Suffering*, p. 49
6. Ibid., pp. 53–54.

7. Kazah Kitamori, *Theology of the Pain of God*, p. 31.
8. D. H. Lawrence, *The Rainbow*, pp. 266–67.

3. Living with Ambiguity

1. Albion King, *The Problem of Evil*, p. 5.
2. Morris Inch, *Paced by God*, p. 40.
3. Inch, *Paced by God*, pp. 45–46.
4. King, *Problem of Evil*, p. 7.
5. Hans Hofmann, *Religion and Mental Health*, p. 17.
6. John Hick, *Evil and the God of Love*, p. 353.
7. James Dolby, *I, Too, Am Man*, p. 9.

4. Learning from Tradition

1. William Ward, *Out of the Whirlwind*, p. 55.
2. Hugh Hopkins, *The Mystery of Suffering*, p. 88.
3. Paul Tillich, *Systematic Theology*, II, p. 66.
4. Leo Tolstoy, *Resurrection*, pp. 250–51.
5. Ward, *Whirlwind*, p. 65.
6. Marc Oraison, *Being Together*, p. 157.
7. Abraham Heschel, *God in Search of Man*, p. 3.

5. Countering Prejudice

1. Victor Reichert, *Job*, p. 108.
2. B. A. G. Fuller and Sterling McMurrin, *A History of Philosophy*, p. 103.
3. Joachim Jeremias, *The Problem of the Historical Jesus*, p. 21.
4. Morris Inch, *Christianity Without Walls*, p. 20.
5. George Buttrick, *God, Pain and Evil*, p. 19.
6. C. S. Lewis, *Surprised by Joy*, p. 230.

6. Cultivating Faith

1. Morris Inch, *Paced by God*, p. 78.
2. John Middleton, ed., *Gods and Rituals*, p. 22.
3. Dietrich Bonhoeffer, *The Cost of Discipleship*, p. 69.
4. William Fitch, *God and Evil*, p. 167.

5. Berakhot, 5a. *The Babylonian Talmud.*
6. *The Interpreter's Bible*, III, p. 1129.
7. Albion King, *The Problem of Evil*, p. 13.
8. Leslie Weatherhead, *Why Do Men Suffer?* p. 163.
9. Ibid.

7. Self-Acceptance

1. C. S. Lewis, *The Problem of Pain*, p. 99.
2. Anton Boisen, *Religion in Crisis and Custom*, pp. 99–103.
3. A. Graham Ikin, *Victory Over Suffering*, p. 38.

8. Devotion to God

1. Edgar Dickie, *God Is Light*, p. 41.
2. Leslie Weatherhead, *Why Do Men Suffer?* p. 162.
3. Hugh Hopkins, *The Mystery of Suffering*, p. 15.
4. Wayne Oates, *Religious Factors in Mental Illness*, pp. 170–71.
5. Richard Sternbach, *Pain: A Psychological Illness*, p. 84.
6. Kazah Kitamori, *Theology of the Pain of God*, p. 63.
7. Hopkins, *Mystery of Suffering*, p. 51.
8. George Buttrick, *God, Pain and Evil*, p. 228.

9. Ministry of Reconciliation

1. Hans Küng, *The Church*, pp. 380–81.
2. Albion King, *The Problem of Evil*, p. 121.
3. Leslie Weatherhead, *Why Do Men Suffer?* p. 127.
4. William Ward, *Out of the Whirlwind*, p. 110.
5. James Sellers, *When Trouble Comes*, p. 121.
6. Ward, *Whirlwind*, p. 112.

Bibliography

The Babylonian Talmud. Thirty-Five Volumes. London: Soncino, 1952.

Bernanos, George. *The Diary of a Country Priest.* London: Macmillan, 1937.

Boisen, Anton. *Religion in Crisis and Custom.* New York: Harper, 1955.

Bonhoeffer, Dietrich. *The Cost of Discipleship.* New York: Macmillan, 1963.

————. *Creation and Fall and Temptation.* New York: Macmillan, 1959.

Buttrick, George. *God, Pain and Evil.* Nashville: Abingdon, 1966.

Dickie, Edgar. *God Is Light.* New York: Scribner's, 1954.

Dolby, James. *I, Too, Am Man.* Waco: Word, 1969.

Fitch, William. *God and Evil.* Grand Rapids: Eerdmans, 1967.

Fuller, B. A. G. and Sterling McMurrin, *A History of Philosophy.* New York: Holt, 1955.

Heschel, Abraham. *God in Search of Man.* New York: World, 1959.

Hick, John. *Evil and the God of Love.* New York: Harper, 1966.

Hofmann, Hans. *Religion and Mental Health.* New York: Harper, 1961.

Hopkins, Hugh. *The Mystery of Suffering.* Chicago: Inter-Varsity, 1959.

128 My Servant Job

Ikin, A. Graham. *Victory Over Suffering.* Great Kneck: Channel, 1961.

Inch, Morris. *Christianity Without Walls.* Carol Stream: Creation House, 1972.

_____. *Paced by God.* Waco: Word, 1973.

_____. *Psychology in the Psalms.* Waco: Word, 1969.

The Interpreter's Bible. Twelve Volumes. G. A. Buttrick, ed. New York: Abingdon-Cokesbury, 1952.

Jeremias, Joachim. *The Problem of the Historical Jesus.* Philadelphia: Fortress, 1964.

King, Albion. *The Problem of Evil.* New York: Ronald, 1952.

Kitamori, Kazah. *Theology of the Pain of God.* Richmond: John Knox, 1965.

Küng, Hans. *The Church.* New York: Sheed and Ward, 1962.

Lawrence, D. H. *The Rainbow.* New York: Modern, 1915.

Lewis, C. S. *The Problem of Pain.* New York: Macmillan, 1962.

_____. *Surprised by Joy.* New York: Harcourt, Brace, 1955.

Madden, Edward and Peter Hare. *Evil and the Concept of God.* Springfield: Bannerstone, 1968.

Middleton, John, ed. *Gods and Rituals.* Garden City: Doubleday, n.d.

Oates, Wayne. *Religious Factors in Mental Illness.* New York: Association, 1955.

_____. *The Revelation of God in Human Suffering.* Philadelphia: Westminster, 1959.

Oraison, Marc. *Being Together.* Garden City: Doubleday, 1971.

Phillips, J. B. *Plain Christianity.* New York: Macmillan, 1955.

_____. *Your God Is Too Small.* New York: Macmillan, 1956.

Reichert, Victor. *Job.* London: Soncino, 1946.

Sellers, James. *When Trouble Comes.* New York: Abingdon, 1960.

Spann, J. Richard, ed. *The Church and Social Responsibility.* New York: Abingdon-Cokesbury, 1953.

Stenson, Sten. *Sense and Nonsense in Religion.* Nashville: Abingdon, 1969.

Sternbach, Richard. *Pain: A Psychological Analysis.* New York: Academic, 1968.

Tillich, Paul. *Systematic Theology.* Three Volumes. Chicago: University of Chicago, 1951.

Tolstoy, Leo. *Resurrection.* New York: Scribner's, 1922.

Ward, William. *Out of the Whirlwind.* Richmond: John Knox, 1958.

Weatherhead, Leslie. *Why Do Men Suffer?* New York: Abingdon, 1936.